WHEN AN ANGEL INTERVENES

Jim Atkisson

Street Light & Story Press

Published by Street Light & Story Press
https://streetlightandstory.com

The Most Beautiful People

The most beautiful people we have known are those who have known defeat, known suffering, known struggle, known loss, and have found their way out of the depths. These persons have an appreciation, a sensitivity, and an understanding of life that fills them with compassion, gentleness, and a deep loving concern. Beautiful people do not just happen.

Elisabeth-Kubler Ross

July/8/1926-August 24/04

Suicide & Crisis Lifeline

Text or Call 988

Help is Available, Speak with Someone Today

988lifeline.org[1]

1. http://988lifeline.org

This is a true story. It contains a narrative some readers might consider triggering. This story contains moments of child abuse, and a graphic suicide attempt narrative.

Friday
1/24/86

;

It wasn't the end;

Chapter One

Opening the closet door, Bill had a difficult time deciding what shirt he should wear. The weather forecast was calling for snow showers, and lows in the twenties. He decided to wear a white shirt, blue tie, and slacks. He was feeling anxious, and a little grouchy.

Bill stood in front of a mirror, and nervously tried to tie the perfect knot for his tie. Over, and over, Bill fidgeted with the tie. He was starting to curse under his breath as he struggled over a "*damn knot!*"

His wife Erika loved this particular tie on him. She said it flattered his blue eyes. He took his jacket off the hangar, and checked it for wrinkles before laying it flat on the bed. Down the hallway, not far from the bedroom, Bill heard the sound of Erika's hair dryer as she rushed to get ready for their big night out! Reaching under their bed, Bill pulled out a pair of black dress shoes, and grimaced at the fine coat of dust on them.

"It's been awhile," he said as he cleaned them off.

He rarely used them, and it showed, but it was time to dust them off, because tonight was his twenty years high school reunion. He heard Erika's hair dryer abruptly shut off, because of an overloaded circuit breaker! She was irritated, and equally frustrated as she rushed around. They were both frazzled by the moment. They were running late, and now she had to configure the circuit overload, and turn the hairdryer back on.

"Tick Tock!" She yelled from down the hall. "We're running late Bill!"

"We're fine, besides, I hear the 'wetlook' is making a comeback this year!" Bill shouted back.

"No. I'm a mess, and I'm not going tonight with wet hair Bill. Please, when Belinda comes over, will you do me a favor, and ask her to run back over and grab her hair dryer, just in case this one is dying? It's older than dirt..." Erika said, as her voice trailed off.

Bill was broke.

Business was slow.

He didn't want to ask the next door neighbor if they could borrow a cheap appliance. He had his pride after all! Money was tight right now, and he felt like everyone in the neighborhood was judging him for an economic downturn. He knew they weren't, but his house was the only house on the street without the latest Christmas fads for decorations.

"Please," Erika insisted. This was not a question, or a request.

"Okay," he said. "I'm sorry things have been slow at work, but business will pick back up soon."

"I don't doubt it," Erika said as she continued to get ready. "We'll get through it. We always do."

Bill felt uneasy about their plans. His anxiety was palpable, and it was weighing heavily on him. Asking their neighbor for another favor, however minor, felt like too much. Lately it felt like life was coming at Bill faster than he could keep up.

He felt like he was drowning...

He just wanted the night over, but he felt compelled to see the night through, and make an appearance at his high school reunion.

"This is supposed to be fun? Isn't it?" he questioned himself.

It was twenty years ago since he walked away from those people, and the other things haunting his memories. It was not a good time in his life. One marriage counselor said he had, *"Post Traumatic Stress Disorder,"* but what did she know he scoffed at himself as he continued to fidget with his tie.

From the corner of his eye Bill saw what appeared to be someone fleeing the scene of a crime. He saw incriminating evidence in the hand of his two year old son as he ran down the hall with a bright red marker.

"Beau has a red marker, and the cap is gone!"

"Where did he get the marker from?" Erika shouted back. "I don't have time for this, please go see if he put any marks on the wall. I need help with the kids..."

The doorbell rang.

"There's the calvary!" Bill shouted from the bedroom as he put his shoes on, and tied the laces.

"Remember to ask for the hair dryer!"

Bill sighed as he looked at himself in the mirror again. It was annoying. He didn't know why he was so bothered by this small request. He knew Belinda would rush back home, grab it, and bring it back with a cheerful accommodating smile. Maybe it was just his overall anxiety, because he was coming face to face with ghosts from the past.

"...triggers," the marriage counselor said.

Bill remembered feeling some denial when the counselor said he had triggers. He disagreed, because twenty years was a long time to put things behind him.

"Okay, I'll ask her," He said as he smiled when he saw his little boy proudly brandishing his new treasure. His hands and arms were red.

"I see where Beau was coloring..." Bill said. His son made his heart glad. The walls were a mess, but with a little, or a lot of elbow grease...he would clean them off tomorrow.

"Can you clean him up before we leave? I don't want to leave him like this, and expect Belinda to clean him up. Oh, did you see where he got that marker from?"

Bill had a reasonable suspicion where the marker came from. All he had to do was follow the red lines on the wall, back to the crime scene.

The squiggly red lines pointed him back to his sister's bedroom. *"This might require more than elbow grease,"* he thought.

He removed the marker from his son's hand, and picked him up gently, "Come with me, you little felon, you made quite a mess for dad"

The doorbell rang again.

"Can you answer the door?"

Bill laid the marker down, and threw a towel over his shoulder so he could clean the marker from Beau's hands, and headed towards the front door.

He could hear Erika ask their daughter if she would put all of her markers away for the night? Their daughter Autumn needed some supervision with them, and at the minute their home was chaotic.

Autumn was busy drawing farm animals on a large sheet of paper. Her grandmother delighted in spoiling her grandchildren. Despite feeling inadequate right now, he was grateful his kids never seemed to do without, because of her help.

The doorbell rang a third time.

"Are you going to answer it?" Erika asked.

Bill felt like he was getting pulled in so many directions.

"When was the last time you checked on Christian?" She asked him as Bill jogged down the hallway towards the front door.

"It was quiet. Too quiet. Were there more crimes, crimes yet to be discovered?" He thought.

"I'll check on him in a moment," Bill said as he paused before opening the front door. The apprehension, and gloom hanging over him like a dark cloud was stealing his joy, and contentment. He wanted to stay home, skip this reunion.

"Nothing good could come from this," he thought.

He surveyed his living room. It was a mess. It reminded him of his life. A cluttered, haphazard mess. There were discarded toys, and discarded sippy cups. Folded laundry in a laundry basket, and their dog was standing on the dining room table.

"You could have at least barked. Now get down!" he snapped harshly, and motioned at their dog to hop off the dining room table.

It was winter. Winter meant prolonged bouts of cold weather, and snow was starting to fall faster than the weather service predicted. The snow afforded a good excuse to stay home, and though he wanted to avoid the night, he felt compelled to go.

Bill opened the door.

"Hi, I'm really sorry for keeping you!" Bill said as he greeted their neighbor.

"No worries, I haven't been waiting very long," Belinda Wilkerson said as she greeted Bill with a warm, neighborly smile.

"It's really chaotic around here, Belinda. It's not too late to turn around," he joked as he swung the door wider to welcome her inside.

"Oh stop, I'm so happy I could help."

"Well, Erika and I appreciate it. Thank you."

"Not another word. You two need to get out more often, but I understand. You guys have your hands full, but you two kids get out and have fun tonight. Have a few adult beverages, but be careful."

"We certainly will," Bill said.

He smiled.

Good neighbors were a blessing.

"I made cookies for the kids," she said as she handed Bill a plate of warm, sweet smelling chocolate chip cookies.

He smiled. His hands were full. Beau in one arm, cookies in the other, a small defiant and hyperactive dog on his dining room table, and red marker on the walls upstairs. Unpaid bills were piled up somewhere, waiting for his attention. His life felt just like his living room right now...*chaotic.* Overwhelming.

"Hey, I almost forgot. Erika's hair dryer keeps tripping the breaker. It's a fossil...she wants to know if she can borrow yours?"

"Say no more Bill. I'll run back home, and get mine lickety-split!"

"Hello Belinda," Erika yelled from atop of the staircase.

"Hey girl!" Belinda shouted back. "Sit tight sweetie. I'll run back home, and get my dryer before you can count to ten!"

"Thank you girl, and please take your time!"

"Nonsense, I'll be right back!" Belinda shouted, waved, and jogged in the direction of her house.

Bill watched a moment as she trekked through the falling snow. It was starting to stick to the grass. The brown, wintery dead grass. Bill disliked winter. Many of his *triggers* were centered around winter. The smell of cold air. The feeling of a wintery breeze.

Bill closed the door on winter for a moment—feeling grateful for his neighbors. They made their corner of the world a nicer place to live. Going back upstairs he heard Erika ask him for help in their bedroom.

"Bill, will you please come and help me get my shoe box? I can't reach it.."

Bill reached high into their closet to grab Erika's shoebox, but without warning, he winced in pain as an old, faded scar tore at him just enough to remind him of the past. The white hot sensation forced him to pause, and use his hand to splint the painful scar next to his heart.

Bill winced in pain, and sat down on the edge of the bed as he massaged the old scar until the pain subsided.

"I'm sorry your chest is really bothering you," Erika said softly as she paused, took time from getting ready, and sat down next to Bill to comfort him. She rubbed his back gently.

"That one really bit me," he said as he continued to massage the wound.

"Did you take something for the pain?"

"No, it just acted up. The cold, and snow always seems to aggravate it. I should be used to it by now."

"I don't know. How does anyone get used to the pain from that? Are you sure you're up for it?"

"I'll go take some aspirin for the pain, but yes, we're going."

"Okay," she said as she kissed him on the forehead. Erika got up, and went down the hall to finish her makeup.

On cold wet days, the scars were a trigger. The bullet wound reminded him he should feel grateful to be alive, everyday.

"You're lucky you're alive..." a surgeon told him once.

Bill went downstairs and got two aspirin. He shooed the dog off the table.

"I'm almost ready!" Erika yelled from upstairs. "As soon as she gets back, we can pretty much go as soon as my hair is dry. Why don't you go start the car, and warm it up for us?"

"The snow is really starting to fall," Bill said as he looked out the kitchen window.

"We'll be fine. We need a night out, but I know you're feeling on edge. Maybe running into some of your old friends will help?"

"I doubt it," he said flatly. He didn't want to leave his bubble. There were ghosts waiting for him.

"Bill, you have triggers...post traumatic stress disorder," the counselor reminded him during his sessions last year. Bill just stopped going. Confronting trauma in therapy, why bother? Why dredge stuff up from twenty years ago? It was a long time ago. He was fine.

"Reunions can be awkward under the best of circumstances for a lot of people, but in your situation, a lot of bad things happened, so it's understandable why you're on edge."

Bill nodded.

"I don't think we should plan on staying for very long,"Erika said.

"Sometimes the past feels like it's near, close enough it feels like it's happening just outside of our front door. Like if I look over my shoulder fast enough it's looking over my shoulder. I don't want to accidentally see anything again."

"I'm trying to understand. You've been on edge for days now. I see when the nightmares bother you at night. You stopped going to therapy, so that didn't help with things."

"I'm sorry. I'm no good Erika. I just feel down right now."

"Well, do you want to do this now?"

"No, I'm sorry. I'll go start the van."

"I love you," Erika said as she smiled.

Bill didn't understand why he felt so defeated, and inadequate. He felt like a failure now. Familiar, critical voices from the past tore away at his sense of value as a man, and father.

"I'm sorry," he said. "I don't mean to sound so down. Maybe I'll call the counselor next week, and schedule myself a session?"

"I think it might help," she reassured him.

The doorbell rang again. Bill rushed to put his coat on, and went outside to clean the car off from snow, and warm it up.

Bill thanked Belinda for everything as they passed one another in the doorway.

Stepping outside into the fresh, cold air with a broom to sweep the dust off their car, Bill rubbed the nagging, stinging pain next to his heart. He climbed into his car, and grimaced as it struggled to start. It needed a new battery.

"One more thing. Why can't I catch a break?"

He grimaced in frustration. It was logical of course, cars need batteries to start, and all batteries had a shelf life, but business was just slow. Slow business meant fewer commissions for him. Fewer commissions meant unreliable car batteries, and old-as-dirt hair dryers became mountains, instead of molehills.

Business, and sales would pick back up in the spring, but for now they would have to hang on for a couple of months. His scar was really throbbing. He sighed from the discomfort. Maybe his body was talking to him?

"...avoid the moment. Stay home in my bubble!" his anxiety was trying to warn against leaving his safe bubble.

The engine started, *"That's a plus...I won't have to ask for a jumpstart right now."*

He watched the snowflakes. Peaceful.

"*...this is a mistake. I don't want to be around people right now.*" It was too late to back out. He wanted to stay home, safe, warm, and with his family.

"*...avoidance,*" the counselor said during one session. It was one of his symptoms, something she wanted to help him work through, but he stopped going abruptly.

"*...I'll call Monday.*"

The windshield wipers brushed the falling snowflakes away. Sales fell off during the holidays. It happens every year around Christmas.

"*...it's called life, but why does it feel like it's a struggle to put one foot in front of the other?*"

Bill knew he had every reason to feel grateful, but the nervous anxiety he felt was starting to wear on him. He was just minutes away from possibly confronting his ghosts from the past, and it was causing him to feel critical of himself. Bill patted the dashboard, thankful the car battery did the job.

Bill was in sales. He sold things. It was the one career he had, where no one held his past against him. The only thing that mattered to his employers? Sales. Closing the deal. Get the sale! No one cared he had a bullet scar next to his heart, a scar he put there intentionally.

"*...I couldn't hide the bullet scar from the recruiter. He said the Army wouldn't take me. Suicide, disqualified me, but my sales manager doesn't care.*"

He wanted to join the Army, help others in law enforcement, but they said, "*No thank you,*" when they saw the wound that almost took his life.

"*...they slammed the door on me.*"

It wasn't the first time, or last time doors were slammed shut, because of an old scar. It was objectionable by social standards to have a scar from something he did intentionally, but few ever really asked, "Why?"

"...I'm alive."

The snowflakes were peaceful, and he was in no hurry to let the moment go. He watched Erika come outside, and wave, "Goodbye" to their babysitter and their kids. She ran delicately to the car, careful to not slip, but fast enough to try and avoid the falling snow.

She got inside, and shut the door. She checked her makeup, and smiled at Bill.

"How does your body feel? Are you still in pain?"

"It feels better," he said. He wasn't being honest. He was feeling the sting from the scars.

"Did the car start okay?"

"It was slow starting, but it won't leave us stranded tonight. It needs a new battery, but lucky for us, they're inexpensive."

Bill backed out of the driveway, and started cautiously driving towards their destination.

"Are you sure that's all it needs?"

Bill nodded as they passed the plow trucks as they worked to keep the roads cleared of falling snow. He felt the shadow of the past encroach more, and more on him with every mile he drove away from the security of his bubble. The night felt cold, dark, and unforgiving. Despite the unfavorable weather, the roads were busy with Christmas shoppers as they made their way to the stores, and malls.

"Terrible time for a high school reunion. It's Christmas, who has a class reunion in the height of the season?" Bill complained.

Erika said nothing. She was trying to avoid feeling annoyed, but she felt the tension.

Bill frowned as he snapped at another driver, "Dim those headlights pal!"

He wanted to close the curtains on his past now. He didn't want to risk seeing something. He wasn't sure what he was afraid to see, but if he saw it, he would know.

"...triggers," the therapist tried to tell him about the triggers. Those emotional connections that tricked his brain into believing a past threat was imminent. She tried to help him learn grounding techniques to manage his flashbacks, but Bill left his therapy behind under the pretenses of excuses. He tried to remember some of those grounding techniques as he turned up the radio.

"Bill. You look like you've seen a ghost," Erika said after several miles of silence.

"You're right Erika. I'm afraid of the ghost."

"I know you don't want to go, but if we did a U-turn right now, and went home...well I don't think that would help."

"I don't want to go, because nothing good can come from looking at my past. I don't want to provoke the ghost."

His scars were starting to scream at him. His body was telling him to run, run away from the perceived danger.

"...my brain is trying to protect me from something that's not there. Fight, or flight?" he remembered learning that during a few of his sessions.

"I'm sorry, but we need you to get help, we can't be held prisoner of the past," she snapped.

"I'm afraid," he admitted to her. It's the truth, and it surprised him he said it.

"...now we're getting somewhere," he thought.

"What are you afraid of?" she asked.

"I'm afraid of seeing," he answered.

He drove slower than necessary as he felt his mood turn darker with every mile. He gripped the steering wheel, and fought the urge to do a U-turn, and drive back to the safety, and security of his bubble.

"I'm not sure I understand you Bill. I guess I underestimated how troubling this is for you. I feel you're on the verge of a panic attack."

"No, I know you don't understand, because no one understands."

Bill also understood he wanted to *feel normal.* This was supposed to be a fun night out with old friends, people he hadn't seen in decades, but that was the very reason why this was triggering. His body, and brain were trying to reason with him to close the curtains, and not look just in case he saw something!

"You don't have to snap at me. I really hope you aren't going to be this irritable tonight," Erika said as she crossed her arms and sat in silence for the rest of the drive.

He sighed.

He was harsh with her.

"I'm sorry."

For now, she stood defiant behind her crossed arms. The rest of the drive remained uneventful, until they arrived at their location.

His old high school.

The shadow of the school peered through the murky night. It looked like a sleeping, menacing behemoth from antiquity as Bill stood before the bare, open windows from the past. The building looked the same to him, as the day he last saw it, but instead of a happy place, it looked like it was glaring at him from a dark dimension. A place where the ghosts from the past wandered the halls.

"We're here," Erika said quietly as they pulled into the parking lot.

The parking lot was cleared of snow, and slush as Bill pulled into an empty parking space. He shut the engine off, and sat in stone silence with Erika as he watched the snow fall again for a few minutes.

"...this isn't normal. I shouldn't feel this much fear over something so harmless. I'm calling for an appointment on Monday. I need to talk to someone."

Erika lowered her arms as she looked at Bill.

"I'm sorry too. I know this is tough. How are you feeling?"

"I'll be okay."

Erika had a relatively uneventful childhood. She had a difficult time relating to Bill's trauma, but she tried. The tension between them was as thick as a heavy, hot, humid day. After eighteen years of marriage, he had the sense to know when she was hurt, or annoyed. This wasn't her fault, and he was responsible for his mental health. He wished he could find the words to adequately express why he was afraid of *seeing something,* because there wasn't anything actually there, but his brain didn't care. It was telling him to run, and fight a perceived threat.

He knew he had to go inside. Cross the threshold, and risk stepping into the past, but still Bill resisted.

"Hey. I have an idea, let's go find some tucked away, hidden restaurant, and enjoy a more intimate dinner? Some place decorated with Christmas lights, how does that grab you?"

"It's getting cold in here Bill, and I'm ready to go inside," she said flatly.

"I just thought the real purpose of our night was to go out for the night, and possibly get our dinner from someplace other than a drive through?"

He felt defeated. So close to his triggers, he felt a familiar harsh message. A critical, condemning voice he had not heard in decades. He felt he had little to show for his life. The threat of *daytime-nightmares* lurked below life's ebb, and flow. Those unpredictable triggers could flood him with terrifying memories, phantom sensations, and often momentarily disorienting reality. The foggy, menacing edifice of the school appeared to be staring back at him. He was worried the building was a minefield of emotional triggers, triggers that would not hesitate to blow up on him, if he strayed carelessly over one.

"I'm cold," Erika said.

She was beginning to fume.

Frustrated.

Two choices, turn around and go home, or walk over the threshold and face the past.

He nodded.

It shouldn't be this hard.

"Okay, let's go in."

Chapter Two

A heavy, strong metallic odor of fresh paint stung Bill's nose as he walked through the school's front door. The phantom odor triggered a menacing relic from the past.

"...They were always painting the lockers," Bill remembered as he stood in the foyer, and smelled fresh paint. There was no evidence of fresh paint, defying a quick observation to even the casual observer, because the lockers were actually dented, and worn.

"...no one is actually painting lockers," Bill argued with himself about the phantom smell. Despite feeling frigid, and removed from reality, Bill's sense of smell argued against what his eyes were telling him. His sense of smell was lying to him. Warning him of something that wasn't there. He glanced around at the other alumni, and their guests, but no one seemed to notice the heavy, sweet smell of fresh, green paint.

He remembered their principal insisted on running a *tight ship,* and believed there were lockers *always* in need of fresh paint.

",,,those miscreant, rebellious kids are always drawing profanity on my lockers!" Bill could hear the former principal bellowing in the hallways whenever he saw the slightest locker defacement. This was a different era, an era where teachers, and faculty were a little more bellicose with unruly students, but despite decades in the past, Bill could hear the echoes of their voices. He prowled the hallways in search of tardy, truant, and mischievous students. He was quick with his detention notes, ready to hand them out like a traffic cop handing out speeding tickets.

As the alumni mingled in the halls, none of them were aware of the phantom smells, and the voices of the ghosts now long gone. He tried to ground himself in the present, and find things that he knew were true about the present moment. Things that he could see, things that he knew he could hear, things he could touch, anything he knew true about reality as he stood next to Erika.

A small line of alumni, and guests formed as they eagerly waited their turn at the registration table. A few of them hugged, laughed, reminisced with old acquaintances, but Bill was removed from them as he nervously anticipated former teachers to manifest like apparitions, and insist everyone to stop, *"Dilly-Dallying"* and get to their class!

From beyond the sound of alumni conversations, Bill heard the distinct din of slamming lockers, rushing students, and frazzled teachers, and all of the commotion was lived out in the span of one episodic flashback. Though he stood in a polite, orderly line at a registration table, he sensed his body was being pressed on by an unseen crowd of bodies running frantically to class.

"...no one wanted a tardy slip from Mr. Shipp." This made Bill smile, just a little as he remembered the stern principal. Though he was firm, and someone you wouldn't want to cross, he was still a good man. Fair. Principled, but when a student was suffering, Mr. Shipp was there to extend resources.

Bill felt triggered by the ongoing rat race of phantom students, just as he would when he was 16. He felt their energy pass through him as Erika stood quietly beside him, unmoved, unknowing to a trapped moment inside of Bill.

"...you need to process Bill," the therapist reminded him during sessions.

Bill felt like he saw a ghost. He wasn't feeling some mild social anxiety, but worried he was on the precipice of a breakdown from all of the emotional flooding.

"...Post Traumatic Stress," the therapist diagnosed him.

He regretted coming, and he wasn't sure how he would make it through the night at this rate, but he planted his feet, and reminded himself, there wasn't anything about that night that could harm him. He was safe. Erika was next to him. He could smell her perfume, and he reached for her hand to hold it, and feel it. It felt like he just stepped off a violent spinning *merry-go-round!*

"Do you recognize anyone?" Erika asked him. Her voice sounded far away. He felt her brush against his arm, but the sensation felt out of body, and her words sounded like they were traveling through a muffled pillow.

"*...dissociative,*" he remembered that word from his therapy. He couldn't remember why he did it at times, but suddenly seemed to feel more present with Erika, because he recognized he was engaging in it.

"This will be so much fun tonight!" She could hear dance music coming from the gym. Her mood lifted, Erika was ready to enjoy herself, "I'm so glad we came, but how are you feeling?"

"I'm okay," Bill said as they shuffled closer to the registration table.

He felt sweat forming inside of his collar as he resisted the urge to turn around, and bolt towards the front door. He was stuck now, even if he broke, and ran from this place, Erika was invested in the moment.

"*...I'm safe. This is now.*" He told himself as he smiled at unfamiliar faces. Pretending. It felt like he was turned into a broken radio broadcast. There were moments of static, out of focus images, but suddenly he would see the phantom students and teachers, or smell the unmistakable scent of fresh, green paint.

Chapter Three

IT WAS THEIR TURN TO step forward to the registration table, and check in for the reunion dinner. When Bill read his name tag, he saw *the name.* This name was no longer his name, but a name that belonged to someone else. He felt uncomfortable acknowledging it, but didn't want to create an uncomfortable moment, because to the casual observer, it was of little importance if he wore a name tag with someone else's name.

"Billy."

"Is everything okay?" The unfamiliar voice asked him.

"Yeah. I'm sorry, it's not a big deal, but I started going by 'Bill' when I turned 18."

He felt angry, broken, drained, and the night was just beginning. It was far from over, unless he decided to retreat as fast as he could, far from this place and back to his bubble.

"Oh gee...I'm sorry, but we used the yearbook when we made up the name tags, and we checked it against the RSVP list. I guess none of us picked up on the unfortunate name discrepancy, but I can find you a Sharpie. You're more than welcome to make the correction," the unfamiliar person suggested.

"Oh leave it Bill. I like it, it's cute. I've not heard anyone call you by your nickname, besides I'm not sure anyone will recognize Bill, but they'll remember Billy," Erika insisted.

Bill refused the Sharpie, and slapped the name tag to his lapel.

"I got rid of that name before we met. I don't like the name."

"I'm sure people will more easily connect with Billy," she replied as she held his hand.

"That's what I fear. I'm trying my best to not connect with him, but it doesn't appear to be working."

"We won't stay long, okay? If you're that uncomfortable after we get a bite to eat, we'll slip out."

Bill nodded. He felt like someone who suffers from claustrophobia and someone just pushed them into a closet, and slammed the door shut. Despite begging someone to not shut him inside he felt the door closing with every minute he spent in this place.

The two began mingling with the other alumni. Bill glanced down one particular corridor, and saw the murkiness of the evening roll back into a vibrant, sunlit afternoon.

The sun looked faded, and less vibrant. Like flat soda from the past—still soda, but lacking the sparkling freshness of today.

Like a mirage shimmering in the desert, reality glimmered between past, and present, as students from yesterday mingled not very far from their older contemporaries of today. He felt the pulse, and surge of electricity as forgotten moments of time arced through his awareness. Distant memories blurred, and bled into the lines of the present tense. The veil of things he wanted to forget were illuminated for him to look at as if they were paintings on a gallery wall.

Inside the flashbacks, he heard the jumbled noise of lockers slamming shut as students rushed. Brightly colored spirit banners from another time hanging from ceiling tiles reminding him to, ***"Check his Spirit!"***

The nauseating smell of fresh paint continued to hound his sense of smell. The age of the locker's condition reminded Bill it was a ghost, lying to him, confounding his sense of smell. As far as he could see, the lockers were faded, worn, battered, and chipped. He felt detached, isolated from reality as the effects of the flashbacks worked like a chaotic time machine.

Hidden among the faces of the past, and present stood one figure in particular Bill feared reuniting with the most, but he was in here, ready to reveal himself among the other ghosts from yesterday. He wore his name on his lapel. The boy's eyes hid the despair, and fear he lived with at home. He hid the fear of his plans he made to rescue himself from the things that went on at home.

Bill stood like he was made of stone. Despite the lively celebration going on around him, he shivered at the dread of reuniting with a much younger version of himself. He didn't want to see it. The ghost-like spirit banners hanging in the hallways, banners from yesterday, heralded the significance of what that day meant for his school, but more importantly for Billy. The lines between Bill, and Billy were razor thin as Bill immersed himself further into the reunion's space. The much younger version of himself appeared as an interdimensional being, because the triggers associated with trauma are not bound by the laws of time, and space. The past presented itself without warning, as if it were today's present reality!

Hey handsome, are you okay?" Erika asked him softly as she touched his arm. The gentle touch grounded Bill just enough to bring him back to the present, affording him the chance to escape the harrowing rip current that threatened to feel as if it would drown him.

"No, but I'll be alright. Right now memory lane feels more like an expressway and I'm caught in the middle of it."

"Not fun," she said. "I'm sorry. I should've been more sensitive, but I felt it was worth the risk so we could have a nice night out, and get in touch with the past...but I guess it's flooding you."

"No, you're right. It was unsettling coming here, but I want to be a little normal Erika."

"Don't say that Bill. You are normal. What happened to you wasn't normal."

"You know what I mean," he argued.

"I do, but don't be hard on yourself. What did Doctor Williams tell you?"

"Feel my feelings."

"I understand why you're feeling overwhelmed, and if we need to go, we can."

"I feel like it's been waiting for me to come back. Stalking me," he whispered.

"That's my point, no one should fear the memories of their childhood. It makes me angry, and I wish you would go back to Doctor Williams. I felt like she was helping you work through some of these things," Erika urged him, as she gently stroked his arm.

"I plan on calling Monday," Bill replied as he nodded at a few unfamiliar faces.

"...who's that? Oh, yeah, Mike..." Bill thought to himself.

"Hey Mike, how are you?" Bill said to an unfamiliar face as the man acknowledged each other.

"Hey Billy! You know, another year older brother, where's time gone?" Mike replied.

"I know right..." Bill agreed as he smiled awkwardly.

"Hey, we'll have to catch up later, but I gotta go refill my drink! Don't forget the open bar bro!"

Bill waved at Mike as he ran off to refresh his drink.

"Who was that?" Erika asked.

"No clue."

The crowd was growing as people bumped into Bill, and Erika.

"Are you going to be okay?" Erika asked.

"We won't stay long, but I'll be okay."

"Okay, when you're ready to go, let's go," she said.

"Let's go find our table," as Bill pointed in the direction of their assigned table.

She took him by the hand as they walked through the noisy gathering. The school gymnasium was dressed up to look like it belonged somewhere in the far past. Music from another era played, and entertained with a loud, and lively sound. Gimmicks, and memorabilia from a bygone time added to the ambiance of the evening. Everything about the moment screamed it belonged from a time Bill wanted to forget! Once they found their table, and sat down, Bill left Erika for a brief moment to go visit the bar.

He waded through the gathering crowd as he walked nervously to the bar. Bill felt anxious leaving Erika's side. He felt vulnerable, and the safety of his bubble felt so far away. His hypervigilant awareness tried to predict what was going to happen next, as it argued against the notion he was perfectly safe in the moment. The trauma told him otherwise, he wasn't safe, and he needed to prepare himself to run back to the safety of his bubble.

Finding the back of the line, Bill took a few minutes to take in the old familiar gym as he waited his turn with the busy bartender. High above the polished basketball court a glimmering disco ball cast sparkling lights across the gym, as he watched ghosts from the past run endless laps around the same court, because an overzealous gym teacher believed in pushing his class towards better fitness! The wooden bleachers were pushed back to make room for the cocktail bar, and dinner tables. Streamers, and hand painted signs welcomed the reunion alumni, alongside phantom "SPIRIT WEEK," signs. The once harsh gymnasium lights that cast a bright, unflattering light over gym classes, and basketball games were turned down to provide a warm, inviting glow. The lines between yesterday, and today were porous, and continued to disorient, and undermine Bill's sense of the present as he continued to make random small talk with relative strangers.

The DJ played the top 40 hits from another era. Some of the songs made him smile, and created a positive moment for him to enjoy songs he once played as loud as the speakers would cooperate. Other songs sent shivers down his spine, because they reminded him of what life felt like on the day he intended to be his last. People laughed, and enjoyed the vibe as Bill continued to weather the emotional flood.

Some of the alumni and their guests took the DJ's challenge, making their way to the makeshift dance floor.

"Let's get this party started!" someone shouted, as the crowd whooped and cheered.

The DJ's voice and tunes boomed from the large speakers.

Bill felt the music's vibration in his feet. His skin felt sensitive, and though there were a few songs that made him smile, most just reminded him of what it felt like to just...*survive.*

"...not much has changed," he thought to himself as he watched old cliques reacquaint themselves into their respective hierarchy, and tribes. Old social groups pulled together, and for a brief moment forgot they had not seen one another in two decades.

Like a morning fog burning away with the rising sun, the warm mood lighting, and shimmering disco ball peeled away from the sudden appearance of a mostly forgotten sunny afternoon. To his former classmates, this moment was an obscure day, a day like hundreds of others they shared together over the four years they attended that school. This day was particularly unique to Bill, a day he would never forget. A day of profound significance. The music became muffled, and eventually became largely unheard by him. The tables were gone. The DJ was no older than thirty, and probably not much older than ten on this significant day in Bill's life.

He found himself now standing near a bleacher, the same bleachers were pushed back for the evening, were now packed with a rowdy, spirit filled teenage student body! He couldn't hear the mundane conversations about the stock market, or a prick boss, or someone discussing their recent back surgery, because he heard the happy, chaotic shouting of hundreds of students as they participated in a spirit rally. On this significant day in Bill's life his classmates were riding the crest of a wave of school pride, because they held hometown court advantage over their district rival, and tonight's game would decide if they were moving on to the district finals.

"...they don't remember that afternoon, because they moved on," he thought to himself.

Bill listened to the chants and cheers of the student body bounce off the polished basketball court, reverberating through the gymnasium as the pep rally hit a highpoint in anticipation for that imminent Friday night game. But despite the ruckus, and fervor, Bill remembered his own solemn feelings of despair, and hopelessness, sitting quietly in the crowd as one empty face.

He remembered the plan.

Not another day. Not one more sunrise.

He watched his peers live life.

He wished his life had been different, and he didn't live in daily fear of harm at home. For years he lived in perpetual anxiety, and a heightened vigilant state of mind. His plan was to escape the torment of abuse, but more importantly, he longed to be a member of this tribe of kids who lived their life apparently free of harm.

"...home is supposed to be a safe castle" Bill thought as he wiped his damp eyes and grappled with himself. *"...not now damn it, get it together,"* he remembered there was a compartment, he needed to find it and shove it away.

But, he saw it all with such clarity.

He saw the school mascot run across the polished gym floor as the phantom marching band shook the gym with the school fight song! The DJ's "Classic Top 40 Playlist" competed with the phantom, ghost-like marching band for Bill's attention. The boundaries of reality, and flashbacks blurred, and thinned as Bill did his best to remain polite, and act the part of someone who was enjoying the moment.

He could see where he sat during the pep rally as he had his feet planted in-between two different places in time. The students booed their opponent's paper-mache mascot, but cheered when their mascot punched, and tossed it around the gym. As Bill felt Billy's tears, and broken mind, and heart, he heard the rowdy cheers, and boisterous laughter. The cheerleaders prepped the students for that night's game as an infectious school spirit spread through the wooden bleachers like a brush fire.

Bill recognized himself from the hallway as he entered the school gymnasium. He watched himself as if he were watching a familiar movie, but not a movie he enjoyed watching, over, and over. He knew where he was going to sit as he watched himself find that seat among the happy faces.

...Billy sat down on the bleachers, and watched the other kids, with no emotion.

The final minutes of the school day were ticking down on him, and soon the day would evaporate. The dismissal bell would soon ring, and he would take another fork in the road, as his peers ran out to enjoy their weekend. It would all be over when they returned to school Monday. He planned this fork in the road for many months, but a crisis at home last night pushed him further.

"*...never again,*" Billy thought. He wasn't going to live in fear anymore, and where he was going, they couldn't hurt him anymore. Time weighed heavily on his heart as he counted the minutes. Those few minutes of life were evaporating. Each second was valuable, and he couldn't squander any of them. As the spectacle went on around him, Billy felt a familiar fear of getting on the school bus, and going home, but this time it would be different. There was no reason for him to feel fear anymore, because where he was going he could leave that place forever. The clock on the wall appeared to freeze, unwilling to inch forward, and bring him to the place of resolution, and finality. The years of living on eggshells, interspersed by explosive volatile moments by his father took a toll on both his mind, and body. The chronic anxiety, depression, broke him down, and now he had to flee to what he believed was a better place.

"...I'm leaving today, I'm going to a place he can't hurt me," Billy thought, as he tried to calm his nerves.

Billy's father believed it was best to break his son, so he could mold him into the person he believed he should become.

"I'll either break you, or make you boy," his father reminded him. His methods varied over the years. Sometimes he endured marathon verbal shoutings, or confined to a metal folding chair for hours at a time. The chair was the worst treatment, because it could last for days. Billy's father made him sit in the chair from sunrise to bedtime. The only time he allowed Billy out of the chair was to go to the bathroom, and eat. There were days when he got home from school, and his father forced him to sit in the metal chair, and write out the same sentence until bedtime. This exercise could go on for hours, and sometimes resulting in the same sentence, written out hundreds of times.

"...I will turn in all of my homework on time."

"...I will turn in all of my homework on time."

"...I will turn in all of my homework on time."

On, and on...

On occasion he would hit Billy, and blame him for the blow, because it was his fault for *"pissing me off."*

"...I'll break you boy."

Those words were scorched in his belief system about himself. There was nowhere for him to go for help. He was afraid of retribution if he just blurted out to a teacher, or school counselor what went on at his home. He doubted anyone would believe him. He tried to think of someone safe he could confide in, but there could be consequences if word got back to his father. The consequences terrified him. No, this was his lot in life. No one was coming to help him. He watched the other kids. They laughed, smiled, sang, and talked about their plans for the weekend. He was envious of them, because they were normal, they weren't treated like animals, or live like POWs in their own home.

"...chair time," that's what his father called time in the restraint. It was a chair, used as a restraint.

There was the odd occasion when Billy's father was in a pleasant mood around the house, and lifted the draconian treatment, and allowed him to go to a friend's home. These respites away from his home were a blissful escape from the jail he lived inside. They were also bitter sweet, because it reinforced what he didn't have at home. He saw busy, but kind parents. He saw furniture, instead of restraining chairs.

The clock continued to move forward, indifferent to what that meant to Billy's time on earth. Time didn't matter. Billy chose this day to leave his life. It didn't give him more minutes in one hour, so he could remain safely in school. The plan Billy decided on, began six months ago, on a hot summer day after his father punched him, and called him names, and forced him to do menial work, because he forgot to tell him about the overdue library books. It was the last day of school, and because there were overdue library books, the school withheld his grades, and would not allow him to move onto the next grade.

"...Fucking Loser!" The man yelled at Billy, because of a certain phone call from school on a hot summer day.

Because of accumulating fees and fines—the school would not release his final grades. As a consequence, Billy would not move forward to the next grade. Adding to the trouble, Billy barely scraped through his freshmen year. What no one understood was, school was not a place for him to get an education, or mix, and socialize. School was his safe castle. No one could hurt him when he was in school.

Now, it was summer and it would be a very long, miserable, potentially dangerous summer at home. He knew he would sit for weeks in the metal chair, because of this apparent egregious offense.

It was during those long hot summer days as he sat locked into a metal chair when his mind started exploring ways to be free. He dreamed of taking a journey, and flying to be free. The chair locked him into a metal restraint, but his mind was free to fly. He started considering *suicide,* because as far as he could tell, this act would free him from the shackles of life under that man's roof. He knew he couldn't run away, because he wouldn't get far, and no one was coming to help. Billy had to escape this life. Suicide, appeared to offer him that space to flee to safety.

This moment did not come easy. There were moments of despair as he wrestled over it, and watching the kids during the pep rally reminded him, he wished there was another way, but there wasn't.

Over the past few months, Billy made attempts at taking his life, but no one seemed to notice. No one noticed the cuts on his arms, or his erratic behavior. He created what he referred to as, "Dry Runs." He knew what would take his life, but it was a frightening reality for him to consider, so he attempted other ways to try and get as close to the edge as possible, without resorting to what lay well within reach just inside of his father's gun cabinet.

Time was up, and he could no longer tolerate another day in that realm of suffering, and the intolerable metal restraint known as, *"Chair Time."* Another day of that harm was worse than the consequences of the devices in his father's unlocked gun cabinet. The days, weeks, and months passed as he got off the school bus, and on most of those days he wanted to fall on his knees, and scream, **"Help Me,"** but what would be the point? No one heard him. Billy felt as if he were born as an invisible person, a child that was destined to get punched, and beat down by those who were supposed to love him.

"...why? What crime did I do?" Billy asked himself, *"I was born."*

He lived as an invisible prison, destined to serve time for his crime of being born. His father threatened to knock his teeth out over an occasional lie. Lying was wrong, but he did it to protect himself from life in the warzone.

Forgot a homework assignment? Lie, tell him he didn't have any homework.

Do bad on a test? Lie, tell him he passed, and kicked the can down the road.

Note sent home from a teacher? Throw it away.

He had to protect himself from physical harm, but lying would only elevate the response from the man. Fear and anxiety hampered his ability to learn. Learning simply wasn't the priority, because he was trying to survive. His father never understood, his only motivation was to survive the day, and not thrive, or excel in school. The threats were never idle, or empty, because his father followed through on them. He believed the man when he told him, *"I'll hurt you."*

The decision to take his life, left him with a sense of peace, and finality. It was almost over. The suffering would be behind him soon, because no one could follow him where he was going. He felt removed, and far away now from the inhumane existence that had become his childhood. He wished he could know the outcome of the night's game, but it wasn't meant for him to know.

"...it's time to go," he kept telling himself.

In less than two hours, he would be gone.

He didn't feel afraid.

Despite the odd feeling of detachment from reality, he felt relieved. He would no longer feel the wrath of a man's simmering anger as he took another shot of whiskey.

Sometimes the man, his father, would get creative when he felt triggered, and decided to throw something at him. Plates of food, a stack of papers, tools, and he once swung a chainsaw at home, because Billy put a scratch in his beloved truck. Billy saw the rage in his eyes as he swung the saw at him.

Sometimes, it was best to not duck, because ducking only made things worse. Billy considered there was a silver lining in these moments, because *just maybe,* if a bruise was bad enough, maybe someone would notice, and ask, *"Are you okay?"*

His father's preferred form of *correction, or discipline,* was to humiliate him.

Because, *"If you won't do better, maybe I should treat you like an idiot."*

The man felt it was necessary to create a daily report card. The end of the semester wasn't good enough, and there was always an accompanying sarcastic note from his father to Billy's teacher, explaining the need for the daily checkup. The crude, makeshift piece of paper required Billy to have all of his teachers provide daily feedback as he often stood in front of his peers.

The words his father used in his note were belittling, and yet, the teachers said nothing.

His life was sinking into peril, and no one threw him a lifeline. Billy begged the man to please stop the daily report cards, but it fell on deaf ears, because his *father* reminded him that, *"he was one notch above a loser, and why he was compelled to micromanage him."*

But of everything he endured, the brown metal chair was the worst.

The chair restraint broke him down, and fostered the plans for suicide.

He could not read, nap, and he had to sit for hours. Sunrise, to sunset.

It affected his body. He was wasting away.

He was relieved to go to school, because it saved him from the chair for six hours. A trip to the bathroom felt like a vacation. He created games to entertain himself as he sat in the chair, and looked out of the window.

"...car soccer," was his favorite contrived game he played in his mind. The rules were simple. Cars traveling from the right during a one hour

period of time represented one team, and the cars traveling from the left represented the other team. The winner? Whatever side sent the most cars in one hour, won.

He spent entire days memorizing insignificant details. Anything to survive isolation and confinement. He snuck paper, and found relief in creative writing, but he was always careful to conceal his writing.

One day during *Chair Time,* he found a small plastic box inside of the desk he was forced to sit behind. Though he spent years sitting at the brown desk, he was shocked he'd never noticed the little box before.

"...how come he never saw this before?" Billy asked himself as he opened the small, clear plastic box.

The room was stripped.

A desk.

Chair.

Bed.

Billy was pleasantly shocked that his father never noticed this little treasure trove. It was full of potential. A sudden toy box he could entertain himself and escape the isolating metal chair.

His father ripped the room bare. Tore things off the wall and shelves. Jamming his finger into his chest, yelling, *"follow the straight and narrow!"*

He opened the box with care.

It was impossible to know how many days, and hours he had sat behind this desk.

Today was not the first time he had opened the desk drawers.

Today was the first time he noticed the white, cigar box.

He opened it with care.

Quietly.

He smiled when he saw the hundreds of different pins. Red, blue, black, white, and yellow pins. Hundreds of them. There were a few odd gold colored pins. These pins were larger than the rest, and only a few, but they had so much potential! This was a gift as he took them out, and organized them carefully on the desk. In his world the discarded, overlooked pins were once used to mark places on a map, but now these pins had another purpose. The large gold pins became instant kings to a lost kingdom, and the other pins became soldiers, archers, and knights as they battled across the desk. The small gift, sent from heaven to alleviate the mental suffering, helped Billy endure the hours of grueling isolation as his body faded away in the forced, metal restraint.

Chapter Four

It was Bill's turn to order his drink from the bartender. He left a five dollar bill on the bar, and waded back through the reminiscing alumni members, and found his seat next to Erika. He was relieved to feel grounded momentarily, back in the present.

Bill could taste his drink.

He smelled Erika's perfume.

He saw the flickering candle on the table.

He could taste the pretzels left as a snack on the table.

He was safe, during this moment. He wasn't sixteen years old cowering in fear of his father. He wasn't planning to flee this life anymore. He was an adult, free to leave an abusive moment if he had too. He wasn't a victim at the mercy of an abuser!

However, immersed in so many triggers, it remained a vulnerable struggle to remain grounded as he sipped his cocktail, and continued to act the part as someone enjoying the moment.

Their table was filled with unfamiliar faces who were assigned familiar name tags. Their table was abuzz with light, friendly conversation, and shared memories as those unfamiliar faces broke out old faded yearbooks, and pictures. Happy memories passed back, and forth among the unfamiliar faces, faces with familiar names as they caught up with one another, and regaled each other about their life experiences.

The voices haunting Billy, were haunting Bill as he measured himself against the perceived success of others. The condemning words, and tones he heard from that man who was bent on *"making, or breaking"* him remained the yard stick, and scale by which he weighed himself.

"...one notch above a loser," Bill heard it clear as a bell. It ripped at his heart, and made him wince. He believed the man who shouted those words in his face as he shoved a condemning finger into his chest.

"...he was right," Bill thought as he sipped the rum.

He tried to focus on the taste of the coke. Taste the rum. Feel the fabric of his shirt in his fingertips. Smell Erika's perfume. He overheard Erika chatting with others around the dinner table.

"...use your senses to ground yourself Bill," the therapist reminded him to help stand firm in the present.

A firm hand abruptly slapped Bill's shoulder. The sudden greeting redirected his thoughts to the present. An unexpected strong smell of whiskey reminded him of his father's daily, *"night-cap"* and made him feel uneasy, but instead of his past, this strong uncomfortable smell was coming from someone he used to know Bill as a friend. Bill preferred rum, because the smell of whiskey made him gag. It reminded him of his father's volatility when he drank whiskey. He tried to smile as he scooted his chair back to greet the stranger.

Once more Bill was connecting with an unfamiliar face, with a familiar name.

"...twenty years will change someone," he thought as he extended his hand to shake the stranger's hand.

The smell of whiskey coming from the man's breath was hard for Bill to endure, but he played the part once more, and ignored his trigger.

"Curt...wow..hey man, it's really good to see you!" Bill stammered as he shook Curt's hand.

Curt ignored Bill's hand and grabbed a big bear hug. The smell of whiskey on Curt's breath was overpowering as the two men hugged briefly.

"...Rum. Beer. Those are safe, but this whiskey is going to make me get sick."

"Billy! I thought that was you man!"

"Curt, wow...it's really good to see you!" Billy said as he flinched again, because someone referred to him by a name he laid to rest the last time he saw most of these people.

"You look great," Curt said with a glassy-eyed, intoxicated smile.

"So do you, so do you ...sooo, what have you been up to Curt?"

Curt pulled a business card from his jacket pocket and gave it to Bill.

"...I work with a large firm on Wall Street."

"Ah. Okay, buy low, and sell high?"

"Bears, and Bulls brother. I buy the dip, and ride the elevator up."

"That's great Curt. I'm glad you're doing well."

"You could say that Billy. I am doing very well...I just bought a new Porsche last week. You know how that goes, right?"

"...sure," Bill said. Lying.

"I got a guy, who gave me a krazzy offer, and it would have been stupid of me to refuse it, so I paid cash for it on a whim. Soo now I got this Porsche sitting in my garage, and I say to myself, 'so now what am I supposed to do with this Fucking thing?' but hey, come on, who can't use a fast car?"

"That's great Curt. I'm glad the markets are good to you," Bill said. He wanted to run to the bathroom, and throw up, and get away from the smell of the past.

"It's a living brother. Some days you make money, and some days you take a haircut, but enough about me, who is this stunning lady with you?" Curt said as he smiled at Erika.

"I'm Erika. *Bill's* wife," Erika said as she shook Curt's hand.

"Oh hey Curt, sorry this is my wife Erika...Erika, this is Curt, we were friends back in the day. We hung out sometimes."

Sometimes Bill's father would soften his draconian, abusive treatment towards Billy, and let him go be a kid. One of Billy's outlets was riding his bike several miles away to his friend Curt's house, and spend the day with him. Sometimes the two boys would meet in the middle, and waist away a lazy summer afternoon climbing apple trees, or reading comic books next to a small pond.

"Erika, it's a pleasure to meet you. Billy, and I had some fun times back in the day. Before we got our driver's license, we used to ride our bikes over miles of dusty country roads."

"I remember those days," Bill smiled as he remembered those imaginative moments as he pedaled his bike, and pretended he was flying a propeller airplane during World War One. It was a safe space for him to imagine the roar of a fierce propeller as it took him high into the clear blue sky, and fluffy white clouds. His imagination rescued him from the prison he lived in most days. As Curt droned on about girls as they pedaled their bikes over the lazy dusty roads, Billy was taken with the notion of having control over a machine that could elevate him high above the war zone beneath him.

Long after Curt went home, Billy's bike became *his aircraft.* He used the bike pedals to maneuver skillfully with the power of his imagination, and fly in, and out of the clouds. From the seat of an imagined open-air cockpit, Billy heard the roar of the engine, and felt the rush of the wind as he ascended high among the clouds, banked, and dived as he pedaled faster, and faster with every mile. He felt safe in the clouds, and loved the feeling of feeling free! Before riding home, he turned his bike sharply on the isolated dirt roads, and conducted dogfight missions against enemy fighters as he imagined what the moment felt like as he embraced the sense of adventure, and living carefree for only a moment. The warm sunshine warmed his heart, and made him smile. In reality, flying above a pretend warzone planted the seed for the need to fly above, and away from the real warzone he lived inside of.

Bill became aware Erika, and Curt were still talking as he drifted back to the conversation, and moment.

"...are you okay Bill?" Erika asked as she touched his arm.

"Oh yeah, I'm good, it's just a real blast from the past," Bill said abruptly as he tried to ignore the nauseating smell of whiskey.

"Billy, and I would ride a couple hundred of miles every summer," Curt said as he finished off his drink, and looked thoughtfully into his empty plastic cup.

"...and drank gallons of sweet tea," Bill smiled as he thought of the refreshing smell of sweet tea. The happy memory gave him a break from the onslaught of whiskey.

He did have some happy memories. Not many, but they were there.

"I feel like today's kids are missing out on moments like that, don't you? Video games, cell phones, are convenient and they have a place, but I think kids are missing out on making memories like we did, because we had to play outside, and use our imaginations to entertain ourselves," Curt said as he looked up from his cup.

"They are missing out. I think some of my happiest memories were ones I just used my imagination, because it got me through some tough moments..." Bill said, realizing he just opened a door.

"I can see that Billy. From what I remember, you had it rough...how are you feeling?" Curt said as he pointed at Bill's chest

"Oh, that...doing well, thank you for asking," Bill lied again as he flinched from the sudden pain of a memory. He missed his bicycle, and the dirt roads he once rode carefree over.

"That was rough. Man, I'm glad you survived, or you wouldn't be here with us today. Erika, your husband was a good boy, no one should have to go through what he did..."

Erika squeezed Bill's hand.

"Remember when we met at Old Man Thurston's farm, and sat next to his pond, and read comic books, and talked about girls?" Bill asked as he tried to close the door he accidentally opened. He wasn't going to address the night he was shot.

"*...It happened during that basketball game. This guy got to go to the game, but I didn't,*" Bill thought as he anticipated the end of this now painful conversation.

"Well, I'm sorry if I brought up anything painful for you old friend, but I hope life is treating you well," Curt said as he looked at his empty cup again.

"I have a lot to be thankful for," Bill responded. He was struggling to feel it now, but it was true.

"That's good to know man, oh hey, let's exchange emails before the end of the night, but I gotta go get another drink before they close the open bar!"

"Sure thing Curt, I would love to," another lie.

"Nice meeting you Erika, take good care of this man!" Curt said as he waved and headed to the busy bar.

Bill watched his old friend for a moment. It was a painful conversation, but it brought back a few happy memories. Only a few brief minutes passed between the two men, but to him it seemed like a lifetime ago when they were flying imaginary airplanes, over an imaginary French countryside. Years before the shooting Billy, and Curt pretended they were flying Dawn Patrol as they pedaled for miles, and miles and talked about life. They talked about cute girls, and music, they kept a sharp eye out for enemy fighter planes. They weren't really riding anywhere in particular, but for Billy it provided freedom from the prison at home.

The dusty roads were now long paved over by the county, and no longer the scene of epic, pretend aerial combat, because isolated country lanes were now replaced by busy subdivisions, and quiet cul-de-sacs. The only testament to their once friendship, and imaginative struggles in the blue sky were a few happy memories.

Bill sat down. He felt sadness. He missed his bike, and the sense he was carefree, and flying, long before he understood what it felt like to experience a shooting. Flying on his bike felt like living. He knew at that moment what he didn't want to see by coming here. He knew exactly why he resisted coming here, because he didn't want to *see* what happened to him after he got home from school on the day of the pep rally.

He twisted a napkin into a tight ball, and though he couldn't see what he believed he feared the most, he saw other ghosts, moments that would lead him to the decision to try and take matters into his own hands to rescue himself, because help never came.

"...it was spring. He was going to make me sit in the chair all weekend, and he made me decide what he was going to do to me," the ghost reminded Bill.

It was Friday, and the weather promised to be gorgeous as Billy hung up the phone after making plans with his friend to ride their bikes all weekend around the Thurston farm. Billy, and Curt were in the sixth grade, and they lived a few miles apart. The two friends made plans to meet in the middle, and spend the day, *"just doing stuff."* The weatherman's forecast promised it was going to feel like Spring all weekend, and all Billy wanted to do was get outside and chase after the warm sun! The days were getting longer, and winter was a distant memory now that Spring had sprung. Billy felt happy for once, and he was looking forward to pulling his bike out of the garage, and getting it ready for the inaugural bike ride towards the farm down the road.

Billy smiled when he felt the anticipation of seeing the imagined view from thousands of feet as he maneuvered his pretend airplane. The long, cold winter made it nearly impossible for him to escape into his imagination as a veteran pilot as he maneuvered his plane in, and out of the clouds, but tomorrow would be the perfect day to ride his bike up into the blue, spring sky.

"I'll meet you at thirteen hundred hours sharp, okay Billy?" Curt said.

"Okay, what should we do for lunch?" Billy asked his friend by phone.

"I don't know, I'll bring fruit, chips, and some other junk, if you make some sandwiches?"

"Okay. Is peanut butter, and jelly good?"

"That's good, can you cut the crust off my sandwich? My mom does that for me. I really hate the crust."

"Okay, I guess...that's just weird," Billy laughed.

"No it's not, but hey my dad wants to use the phone, so I gotta go, but 1 PM at the farm. Okay?"

"I'll be there. The weather is going to be perfect."

"It's already getting warm, I felt it when I got off the school bus this afternoon," Curt said.

"Okay, I'll see you tomorrow," Billy said as he hung up the phone.

As Billy hung up the phone. He felt nervous. Maybe it wasn't such a good idea to make these plans, because he had a reasonable suspicion his father would make him cancel them. He hoped he could just get out and go play with his friend, he really didn't want to spend the weekend doing chores around the house. They were menial, busy work. He picked up sticks, moved rocks, cleaned out a tool shed, or helped him organize his garage. There was always firewood to gather in the woods behind their house. The man always found things for Billy to do, instead of just letting him go spend leisure time with his friend Curt, or go to the mall like the other kids.

He was kicking himself for allowing the charade to go on with Curt, but he wanted to feel normal. Billy knew his father talked about a large pile of rocks he wanted moved, so he could expand his garden in the spring. Billy had been looking at that pile of rocks for weeks, but it was too cold until now to move them around. He felt a lump in his throat, and thought about trying to lay low the rest of the evening. Maybe he could sneak out of the house in the morning, and pedal his bike as fast as he could in the direction of the farm up the road. He sighed. He promised to make peanut butter, and jelly sandwiches. He also promised to cut the crusts off them. So he would certainly draw attention to himself in the kitchen. He worried about his father coming home, as he anxiously looked out the windows.

Waiting on his father to come home was always the worst. Billy tried to anticipate what kind of mood his father would be in. He keyed in on subtle cues as he watched him from his bedroom window.

"...were his footsteps heavy?"

"...did he slam the door when he got home?"

"...what's his body language?"

Billy needed to predict the man's mannerisms, because he felt he always had to engage in some manner of damage control. He feared his father coming home, and today was report card day. He knew there would be hell for him to pay, and he should have just been honest with his friend Curt, and told him he had plans for the weekend, and wouldn't be available. He knew what those grades reflected, and bad grades *always* triggered the man into an abusive rage with him. He knew how these *conversations* went. Billy could feel the dread coursing through his veins. The idea of riding a bike on a beautiful spring day with his friend was far out of reach right now. If he got off lucky, the worst thing that would happen to him was his father would tell him to move rocks all weekend.

An hour after Billy hung up the phone, he could hear his father pull into the driveway. He came inside, and said nothing. He was silent, brooding. This wasn't going to be a good night for Billy.

Dinner came, and he said nothing.

The house was thick with tension, because the man was angry about other things, and so for the moment, Billy wasn't on his radar, or his end of the semester grades.

Billy could hear the tick-tock of the clock as the evening hours progressed without incident. He wanted to go into the kitchen and start making sandwiches for his picnic lunch with Curt, but he knew it wasn't safe. He had to keep his head down like a soldier in a fox hole. Out of sight, out of mind, was cover, and safety. He also wanted to get his bike out of the garage and look over it, but it wasn't safe for him to leave the cover of his bedroom. Billy wondered what the other kids were doing now? What was Curt doing? Were any of the kids from school at the mall right now?

It was hard for him to not cry, but he had to listen for any sound of trouble. It was only a matter of time before the man yelled for Billy to come out of his room and bring his grades with him. He felt like a man living out his final moments on death row. Minutes away from walking to the gallows.

He wished he were making peanut butter and jelly sandwiches, or watching TV, but he needed to prepare himself for trouble: *The moment was coming...He couldn't avoid it...*

"...you piss me off boy," was often how these moments began. If the man didn't say that, odds were good that Billy would escape the moment with only a nominal amount of harm, but if his father started out by saying that? It ended badly. Billy knew he had to remain vigilant, everyday. He had to remain alert, always watching the subtle emotions from the abuser.

...every, single, shift.

He heard his father yell his name. It was time.

He thought of the other kids, and wondered what they were doing tonight?

"...it's such a beautiful night. Perfect night to be outside, or at the mall with friends," Billy thought as he walked into the kitchen.

"All this semester, you had missing assignments?"

Billy nodded. He wasn't sure why he couldn't focus, or concentrate in school, but perhaps it had something to do with the chronic anxiety he felt?

"You piss me off..." there. He said it. Billy was certain he understood what it felt like to stand in front of a firing squad, because here he was.

"You've been deceptive, and lied to me?!?" Oh Christ Billy thought to himself, this is going to be really bad.

"...Jesus, please keep him from hitting me," Billy prayed to himself. But he just used the Lord's name in vain, so he was worried Jesus wouldn't spare him from whatever this man was going to do to him. *"...I don't think God hears me,"* he would often say to himself as he tried to imagine God cared.

"i can't fucking hear you boy! Speak to me like a man when you speak to your father!"

"..yeah, this is going to be bad," Billy thought. He missed Curt. He missed having fun. *"...I think a firing squad would be better."*

"Yes Sir," Billy tried to answer with conviction.

When he started swearing, he knew bad things were going to happen. He knew that somewhere out there, other kids were playing, and spending time with friends.

"Yes sir, what?" the man demanded as he jabbed a finger into Billy's small chest.

"I lied sir," Billy responded, aware he was starting to cry. He couldn't help it, but he was afraid, but the tears *always* made things much worse.

"I'll tell you how we're going to resolve this. We're going to try, and do something different. Tonight, you decide your own punishment. Do you understand?"

"Yes sir," Billy cried. He felt terrified right now, and Jesus wasn't going to save him. He prayed, but Jesus said nothing to help. The other kids were playing, spending time with their friends, but not him. He was invisible, and frankly no one cared that this was happening to him right now.

"Stop fucking crying, be a man! Goddammit you piss me off, if you can't do the time, don't do the crime!" His father roared as he threw his report cards in his face.

"...I knew this would be bad," he thought as he sobbed. He should have just told Kurt he couldn't ride bikes with him tomorrow, because he was supposed to be making a picnic for them right now, not enduring an imminent firing squad.

"Yes sir," he mumbled in-between sniffling.

"Two choices, so you decide, do you want to sit in the chair all weekend, and it starts right now, or do you want a beating. If you take the beating, you won't have to sit in the chair all weekend."

He felt the warm evening breeze coming through an open window. There was still a chance he could still meet up with Curt if he took the beating, but the beating terrified him.

"I'll be outside waiting for your choice. You have thirty minutes, or I'll make it for you, and you don't want that."

Chapter Five

Billy heard the sound of the screen door slam shut as Billy's father went outside. He felt despair over the idea he would have to sit within the confinement of the metal chair, all weekend! His father would make him write the same sentence over, and over, and over again if he sat in the chair.

However, the idea of a beatdown with a thick leather belt terrified him, because these weren't just *spankings i*n the sense of disciplining. They were beatdowns under a rod of discipline, because he had *"Pissed his father off."* Billy often lied to avoid *pissing off* the man, so he could rescue himself from a beatdown, or the chair. Billy knew this was going to be a first order beating, *why wouldn't it?*

It's what his father called them.

"A beating."

This wasn't the first one.

He could remember another instance where his father threatened him with one of these beatings, but Billy thought ahead, and wore an extra pair of pajama pants to provide a cushion against the blows.

However, if he endured the beating, he could make peanut butter and jelly sandwiches, and plan on riding his bike tomorrow! He wouldn't have to sit restrained all weekend, writing the same sentence over, and over, and over again.

"I will do my homework and turn in all assignments."

"I will do my homework and turn in all assignments."

"I will do my homework and turn in all assignments."

The pain of the chair was a slow form of suffering, but the beating would be over in a few minutes. The pain would be severe, but brief, but he could get on with his life when it was over.

Sometimes, the man added a twist of anguish to his method of *discipline. On occasion his father scheduled the beating in advance.* He once told Billy before he left for school, he would feel the wrath of the belt before bed later that night. On another day when Billy got home from school, his father told him before bed at 8 PM he would beat him with the belt before he went to bed. As Billy sat and ate dinner that night he felt nauseated, and he could feel his hands shake as he held the fork. He cried, and begged his father to not hit him with the belt, but there was no mercy, because he reminded him, *"If you can't do the time boy, don't do the crime."*

As he got ready for his fate later that night, he suddenly put on a second pair of pajama bottoms. Would they help soften the blow of the leather strap against his skin? It didn't really matter, because his father changed his mind, because he was busy and just sent him to bed without his *thrashing.*

"..boy do you want a thrashing?"

No. Billy never wanted a beating, or a thrashing with a heavy leather strap.

Though he was spared the harm of the leather belt that night, he felt all of the mental anguish as if he had been hit by the actual instrument his father would tear from his waist and yield it like a whip whenever Billy *pissed* the man off.

"...the chair all weekend,"

Or

"...the beating, but it would be over in a couple of minutes. It'll hurt, but I'll be free."

Those were his options.

Billy got up, and walked towards the screen door. He paused before stepping outside to face the man. Violence waited for him outside, and it terrified him, but sitting restrained in a metal fold up chair all weekend was much worse. Before stepping outside he escaped the moment by mentally removing himself from this reality. He would lean into the moment physically, but mentally he checked out. His father couldn't get at him in the compartment he created in his mind.

"1917, I'm patrolling the skies over France in my biplane. It's dawn patrol, and I'm about to face the hun as they try to eviscerate me, and my wing man over the small farm not far from our headquarters!"

His imagination absorbed some of the fear, and gave him the ability to survive this traumatic moment. Billy was in a dissociative mind cloud as he approached his father. He cleared his throat.

"Dad. I'll take the beating."

There was an irony in calling him "Dad."

"Well, I'm glad to see you taking this like a man today, and not some limp-wristed weakling. Let's go. I'll make it quick boy."

His father wiped the grease from his hands.

He was working on a tractor in his garage. It was dark. It smelled like oil, and grease. It also smelled like saw dust, and old cigarette smoke. This was his father's sanctuary. A place he came to drink his whiskey, and fiddle with odd projects. The "garage" was detached from the rest of the house, and it was a place that made Billy feel uneasy. This was the worst place for him to take this beating, but his step mother, and little brother would not hear, or see what was about to happen to him. It wasn't the first time he'd been beaten with the heavy leather belt, but it would be the first time he bled.

He felt small, and fragile, as he tried to imagine the sweet smell of free air rushing over his face as he maneuvered his airplane above this ugly place, and not smell the pungent odor of stale cigarette smoke, saw dust, and discarded oil.

Billy suddenly felt as if he made a mistake as his father shut the garage door, but it was too late for him to change his mind, and run away from this place. He would have to be brave for the sake of freedom. He couldn't tolerate having his body restrained all weekend in the metal chair.

"Turn around, and lower your pants," his father said as Billy compiled down to his underwear. The thin fabric was all that he had to protect him from the weight, and force of the leather strap. He remembered back to the night when he tried to pad himself with two pairs of pajamas just before a similar "whipping," but he lacked that luxury right now. He could hear the sound of ice cubes clinking around inside of an almost empty glass of whiskey. He felt as if he were going to vomit from the smell of whiskey, and fear. The smell was vile to him, and it would haunt him for many years. He could smell the darkness as his body detected imminent danger as it tried to warn he was at risk for serious bodily harm, but there was nothing he could do to escape it. He detached himself from the moment, and fled deeper into the mental space he created with his mind.

"...this will hurt," his mind said just as he left for that safe compartment.

He watched with a detached reality as he saw his father raise his arm high above his head with the leather belt. He was about to get flogged for telling a fib about some unfinished homework assignments, and misleading his father about his grades for the semester. In reality, he passed, barely, but he passed.

"...please God, make him stop," he prayed to God.

It wasn't the first time he prayed to God, and each time he believed God heard him, but it never seemed to help, because what he got was another day in the metal chair, or another plate of food thrown at him as his father eviscerated him verbally.

The belt struck with ferocity as it appeared to bite into his back, but he held on despite the withering belting. It felt more like a flogging instead of a *spanking* to Billy.

"...Jesus doesn't hear me. He doesn't," Billy cried as he endured another fierce blow, for misleading his father about his academic report

card. The sound of leather cracking as it hit his bare back. The heavy smell of sawdust, discarded oil, and cigarette smoke burned itself in his memory as it formed a traumatic memory, and trigger.

"*...no one loves me,*" his consciousness told him. He was getting flogged right now, instead of making a picnic lunch for himself, and a friend. He was right to believe this, and it would grease the skids for future events. A home should feel safe.

It was almost over, and it was time to focus on the prize. He knew he wouldn't have to sit all weekend in the chair. Despite the burning pain searing itself through his back, he felt optimistic, and perhaps happy! He was proud of himself for choosing his fate at that moment. He took what the man dished out, and he was still standing tall.

Billy overcame his natural fear.

His father was capable of hurting him.

He had a history of it.

But Billy wanted freedom, looked through the moment, and saw the relief of tomorrow.

However, it was also a tragic irony...

It was a foundational moment that led him to a similar resolution a few years in the future. He chose his destiny, not his father. He was originally afraid of the pain, and destruction the *beating* held for him, but the idea of suffering all weekend wasn't something he would entertain. He wanted to fly. Tomorrow Billy would feel the joy of flying in the sunshine, and though he was limited to pedaling a bike on a black top road, his imagination was limitless and if he wanted to fly, his imagination would take him there! He could fly, and the faster he pedaled, the higher he would fly away from this place.

"*...I'll make you, or break you boy,*" the man reminded him all the time, but Billy wasn't breaking. He took punches like a boxer in the ring. His father was trying to break him, subdue him into some sort of perceived obedience, and compliance in school, but Billy lived trying to survive day to day. His back felt like it was screaming at him. It hurt. It was burning. The heavy leather belt made an ugly cracking sound.

Billy used his imagination, and blocked the ugly smells in the garage, and imagined the beautiful, sweet smell of honeysuckle. The same honeysuckle growing along the fences that ran alongside the road where he rode his bike in the spring, and summer. It would smell like that in the morning! It wasn't time for the farmers to cut their grass, but he threw in the smell of fresh cut grass for good measure. His imagination was his friend. He didn't understand why God wasn't intervening, and making his father stop hurting him, but his imagination never failed him. It was always there with him. It could take him anywhere he wanted it too, and it would put a safe wall between him, and the ugly things that went on at home.

He could hear the crack of the leather strap, but thanks to his friend, it didn't feel like it was actually happening to him. His imagination was protecting him like a protective, best friend.

His father could not reach him in the imaginative world he created.

He remembered the little map pins.

Those little map pins the abuser overlooked, allowing him a window of escape from the mental torment of sitting, wasting away, and state at the vastness of an empty wall.

This was his mental safety hatch.

He could smell the honeysuckle and fresh cut grass.

He could feel the warm sun on his face, and the wind rushing over his sweaty arms as he pedaled as fast as his legs would go.

He heard the belt strike him, but it sounded far away!

His friend was next to him.

His friend knew what was happening. He didn't turn a blind eye to Billy.

He gave Billy a free, safe place to run, and play.

Far away.

Billy's father stopped.

"Go inside. Get cleaned up. Don't tell anyone about this. Do you understand me?"

"Yes sir," Billy said as he wiped his eyes. He was now free, because tomorrow belonged to him!

Though this was not the first time he'd been beaten, it was the first time his father ever warned him to not tell anyone about what happened at home.

Billy had a hard time moving his legs. His legs felt rubbery, and unsteady as he walked.

"Go inside, and take a shower right now, and don't say a word," he demanded once more.

Billy went inside, and headed to the bathroom. Once safely behind the bathroom door, he peeled his shirt off, and moaned from the burning, stinging sensation. His back felt like it was on fire. Billy turned his back just enough to catch a glimpse of it in the bathroom vanity mirror. He was bruised, and his back was bleeding from torn skin. Billy felt numb, because this had never happened before, and he felt fear. He realized the fear he always felt for this man was now justified. He'd beaten him to the point it left him bruised, and bleeding.

His father opened the bathroom door, saw his back and again told him to keep quiet.

"Yes sir," Billy replied, meekly, exhausted, and no longer felt happy about riding his bike tomorrow. His back hurt, and it was scary to look at. He felt as if something were broken, violated, something dreadful just happened, and he had no voice to tell anyone what just happened to him.

He took a shower, and winced as the water flowed over the torn, and bruised skin on his lower back. He was now free to roam free in the morning, and he finished showering and went outside to get his bike ready for the morning. Earlier he wanted to make sandwiches, prepare a picnic, but he decided it would be safer to disappear into his room for the night, and get some sleep. Billy didn't trust his father, and he worried, this wasn't over. He felt on edge, but didn't understand why he felt as if he had to sleep with one eye open? He earned the right to be free in the morning, but he just sensed a remaining cloud on the horizon.

The next day's weather was splendid, and the morning sun felt amazing as Billy got himself ready to meet Curt. After a very long, cold winter, the first warm Spring morning made the previous day's torture worth it if it meant he could live this moment outside, and not restrained in a metal device. His back was black, and blue with an open abrasion, but the pain was almost gone. His legs felt strong, and ready to do serious pedaling! Billy felt as if he could ride a hundred miles, even if those miles led to nowhere in particular. The point was to just meander in the sun, and smell the fresh smell of Spring. He was going to pedal a few miles out to an old farm, and meet Curt. There were trees they could climb, a pond to skip rocks, and small hills they could jump with their bikes. If they felt even more adventurous they could explore an empty, abandoned barn, but they were always a little fearful about going in it. Each summer, they promised they would go into the old barn the next summer when it warmed up, but when summer came, they were always afraid the old barn hid snakes, or dangerous dry rot, and it was not safe to climb inside, but it was still a tempting idea to explore.

As Billy packed his lunch, his father wanted to know where he was going?

It felt like an odd question. He remembered the cloud of uncertainty he felt when he went to bed. He felt dread as he paused getting ready.

"I'm going to ride my bike."

"Just you, or that kid that lives down the street?"

"Curt?"

"Yeah, that kid. I don't like him. He's trouble, and I don't want you hanging out with him, besides I need your help around here today."

"But, why?" Billy cried, stammering, confused...

"Because I said boy. I think he's the problem. I think he's the reason your grades suck. I think you need some time around the house to think about the things you did this semester."

Billy felt anger. Confusion. His back hurt. He'd been beaten. He should have just picked sitting in a metal chair for twelve hours on Saturday, and Sunday, and skipped getting beaten by this man.

"But you said yesterday..." Billy stammered, careful to not provoke the man further, but unable to restrain his confused disappointment, and anger.

"You heard me dammit. I need your help moving rocks out of the garden today. I told you I have plans to expand it this summer, and we have chores to do around here."

Those rocks. He knew they were going to come back and haunt him this weekend. He knew he should have just made an excuse, and lied to his friend, instead of pretending he was a normal kid, who lived in a normal house. Billy felt as if he were a prisoner on a chain gang breaking rocks on a rock pile. He felt the tears. He knew better. The tears always made things worse, but not this time. His father ignored them, pretending not to see them. He felt trapped, helpless, and he gave up. He took that "beating", flogging, because his father gave him the power to choose his own destiny, and rewarded him by cheating him the next day.

"...what was the point of it all?" He would have been better off sitting. His father would still insist he spend the day moving rocks out of his expanding garden.

"I don't care what I said," his father went on, "I need your help with the rocks. We need to get them out of the ground while it's warm today. You're one notch above a loser boy, and you need to do better...if you can't do the time, don't commit the crime!"

Billy felt a chain around his ankle as he locked at the old muddy garden.

"...what crime?" but he knew the answer to the question, *"I was born."*

The garden was full of rocks. He knew his father wasn't going to help him move them. There was always something else he needed to go work on. Billy walked over to the wheelbarrow, and past his bike. His father walked past him, and ignored him. Billy felt as if the man just knocked him into a frozen pond, and left him to swim his way out of it. He felt angry at his father.

"...I didn't have to take that beating. I could have just stayed in the damn chair, spared my back, and still carried his rocks all day!"

Billy picked up the wheelbarrow, and began pushing it towards the garden. One by one the rock pile grew as Billy carried each one to the waiting wheelbarrow, and pushed the heavy laden cart over to the designated rock pile. He did feel as if he were in a prison gang as he busied himself busting rocks on the prison rock pile. His father had become the warden of this prison, and Billy knew he had to escape it one day.

He felt himself disconnected with the grief of missing Curt, and their fun filled afternoon, because he'd been beaten, and forced to move a pile of rocks the size of a car. Billy daydreamed of what it would be like to leave this prison, and fly away to heaven.

"...Would it be like riding my bike on a beautiful day?"

"... Would heaven smell like honeysuckle?"

Billy felt like he wanted to die, because dying would be better than this, and this thought...comforted him. These thoughts were the gateway to a decision he would arrive at years in the future, and it was a decision he would regret. But for now, the thoughts gave him false comfort.

Bill tossed the twisted napkin he'd been anxiously twisting in a ball onto his plate.

Bill needed air.

He needed to ground himself, regain his composure, and remind himself he wasn't moving rocks right now. He abruptly slid his chair back from the dinner table, and kissed Erika on the top of her head.

"Are you okay?" She asked.

"Yeah. I need to go to the bathroom, but I'll be right back," Bill said, as he tried to reassure her before stepping away.

He had to get out of this gymnasium, and away from the ghosts.

He walked quickly across the gym floor. He pushed hard against the exit door, and let it slam shut behind him with a heavy **CLATTER!!!**

A few startled people glanced at him as he walked hastily out into the hallway. With the door shut behind him, the noise of the dance music sounded muffled. He felt terrible for leaving Erika behind with people he no longer knew, but she couldn't see the same ghosts he saw. The near empty hallway reminded him of the gates of an old cemetery.

"...tread softly," his brain warned. The gymnasium was not a safe place for him, but now he stood face to face with more ghosts as he walked further into the past. Billy once walked these halls as he planned his final days.

Bill saw yellowed school pictures from bygone generations on display next to trophies from forgotten glories behind display glass. As flickering display lights cast a gloom over the isolated hallway. His heavy footsteps meandered further into the chasm of the past. This was not a highschool, but a mausoleum, and the voices of the past were yelling to be heard from behind the veil of silence as he followed a once familiar path around the building. He decided to go look for his old locker, and wondered if he would be able to remember where it was. Despite the feeling he was walking over the graves of a forgotten youth, it felt good to distance himself from the polite, idle chit-chat going on around the dinner table.

Bill missed his bubble. He missed the safe sounds of the home he knew today. The pang of missing his kids felt acute, as if he'd been kidnapped against his will to live among the ghosts of a decade he almost didn't survive. That *thing, he almost didn't survive...that thing that almost denied him the life he knew today...was lurking near that locker.* Somewhere in the mausoleum of a school, a repository for forgotten memories, was a locker he closed for what he believed was the last time, just an hour before he would do the thing he was so afraid of seeing Billy do.

Bill found the student common area, and nothing about it changed in the twenty years since he left. He was close to it. Close to the locker, and the smell of fresh green paint was strong. It was a ghost, the smell of fresh paint...not reality, but Bill's brain was telling him Billy's locker reeked of nauseating green paint! Bill saw a familiar bulletin board, cluttered with announcements, but these were just nonsensical posts from twenty years ago. The information on the bulletin board, dated, forgotten except within the realm of a flashback! This information was relevant to Billy's peers, but useless words on paper that only served to disorient Bill's understanding of the present day. The flashbacks felt like a stage curtain. Present reality was backstage, obscured from the past by a curtain of time, but Bill felt the lifting of the curtains brought the next act out for him to witness as an unwilling spectator.

Billy dodged his classmates as they clamored through the hallway, eager to start their weekend.

It was Friday, and the school day was over. The pep rally was done. The important basketball game was hours away. There was a lot of excitement, and anticipation as the hallway buzzed with life, but not for Billy. Tomorrow was not to be, because there was no tomorrow for him. In fact, there would be no tonight either. There were only a few hours of time left for Billy, as he closed his locker for the last time. He watched the others embrace life, and living, unaware of the surreal moment for Billy. He was only an hour, maybe two hours away from passing away from this life.

The night of the present, bled into the daylight of the past as Bill felt himself untethered from reality as ghost-like apparitions tore away the curtain separating yesterday, from today! The virulent nature of Bill's flashback manifested a bygone reality in the form of a disorienting unreality. It was very real to him. They weren't hallucinations, because what Bill experienced actually happened to him in the past. He struggled once more to swim against the current of the metallic odor of fresh paint, and now he understood why the smell of fresh paint always made him feel uneasy.

Bill found his old locker.

The locker was the anchor point between the life he was living today, and the life he was willfully surrendering to suicide in the past. It was the last stop in between the kids busy going to, and from, busy living their life, unaware Billy was on his way home to end his life. The final bell of the day rang, dismissing students for the weekend, and the halls were a calamitous noise of voices, banging lockers, and laughter as Billy stood solemnly in front of his locker for the last time. They were all unaware as they walked past Billy they would never see him again.

Over the years Billy, and Curt's interests changed, and they spent less, and less time together. Billy felt alone. Isolated. Friendless, and invisible as he stood in front of his locker. He longed for someone to throw him a lifeline, but when you're invisible, no one knows when you're drowning.

Billy prayed, often, but though Billy felt God wasn't listening, he wasn't ready to abandon his belief in God.

"*...maybe he was just too busy to pay attention to me?*" Billy often thought as he wasted away in the metal chair, or lived another day in fear of bodily harm.

No one was coming to help him.

In the end, his mindset was positioned to accept suicide. He planned for it. Planning his own suicide brought him comfort. It gave him a sense of control over a situation Billy felt as if he had no control, and it offered him the promise, *"everything will be okay soon."*

Billy knew he would just have to endure the valley for a brief moment.

The days of sitting in that cold, metal chair as it broke his back, and spirit were now over. Today he was going to bank, and fly over the clouds, but this time it would be for real. As soon as Billy pulled the trigger to the firearm he intended to use, he anticipated his spirit would soar higher over the clouds than his bike could ever carry him. These were all Billy's unfounded conclusions, because he had never experienced death before, he had no way of really knowing the truth about suicide, and what actually held for him in the coming minutes.

As Bill touched his old locker, he remembered. He remembered the crisis the night before he shot himself on that Friday just over two decades ago.

It was a Thursday.

Report card day. Billy's semester grades.

The semester report cards were always the trigger for the bad things at home...

His semester grades always had the potential to trigger his father's rage against him. As Bill continued to reflect through Billy's eyes, he remembered that particular semester was particularly poor.

"...that Thursday night. The night before the pep rally, and the district championship. I just stood there, and watched in horror as my mother protected my younger brother, because he was afraid of my father."

Billy watched his brother cry in fear. His brother had watched their father rage, and punish him over the years, because of bad grades, and now he had fallen into the same circumstances. Billy understood the fear, and the sense of what it felt like to stand in front of the executioner. Their father would be home soon, and now his little brother would have to face his father.

His younger brother was crying in his mother's arms.

Billy never had anyone to nurture him. This was his stepmother, and his relationship with her was distant. Billy was a chore. A child to feed, take to the doctor, wash his clothes, but nurturing was always directed to his little brother. Billy's mom left when he was a few years old, and he had very little contact with her. This dynamic always added to his sense of feeling alone, and isolated. He never had a mother willing to protect him against his father's abuses. He watched his brother cry in her arms. Billy felt sorrow for his little brother, but he knew his situation was far more bleak than his little brother's. His semester grades were tucked away in his shirt pocket. His step mother was unaware of this. He had a plan.

She was trying to console her son as she asked to see Billy's report cards. Her eyes looked alarmed.

"...where are yours?" she asked.

Billy suddenly felt calm. This was the crisis moment, just before he lit the fuse to a plan. It was a suicide plan he worked out privately in his mind over the past several months. This whole moment was tragic. Billy needed out. He needed to escape this life, and suicide seemed to offer him that escape. He needed to be brave now for all of them. He had to lie. He needed to buy time, and take the focus off his little brother.

He was watching his nine year old brother cower, protected by *his* mother.

Billy was alone.

No one stood for him.

He knew the abuser would be enraged once he saw the collapse in their report cards.

"...did you hear me? Where are your report cards Billy?"

Billy knew she was looking to throw him under the bus, to spare her son.

She was assuming his grades were worse than Billy's, and she was right on that assumption, but he knew he had to lie right now. He could read the room, and he knew if his grades were worse, his father would forget his little brother, because he would be preoccupied with him, or so that is what he imagined he heard within his step mother's questioning.

He had to be brave like he was on the day his father gave him the option of beating him, or sitting confined for the weekend in a metal chair. This moment felt no different to him. His father had conditioned him for this.

"...Billy, for your sake, I hope your grades are better than his, because I would not put it past your father to really hurt you this time," she warned.

It was a threat.

A warning.

It was time.

No more of this.

"...I do not have my grades today. I will have them on Monday."

He was committed now, and there was no turning back from lying. He lit the fuse to the plan. There was no other way, because he was unable to endure the psychological trauma. His brother was afraid. His brother had seen what happened. He had to lie to save himself, and to save himself, Billy believed he would have to die tomorrow.

"...I will have my grades on Monday. Mom...my grades were very good this semester. Don't worry, my father will be proud of me."

His step mother looked shocked, and confused.

"...Why don't you have them today?" She asked.

"...There was a snafu, or glitch, or something in the front office, but they said it'll be okay, and we will have them on Monday."

Billy knew he wasn't a good liar, but he needed to buy time.

The carbon copies of the previous semester were neatly tucked in his pocket, and they were burning a hole in his pants—he needed to stay calm, sell the lie.

Lie his way out of danger.

Stall, and buy time.

The lie was working, because suddenly the atmosphere felt less fearful as Billy watched his brother wipe his eyes, and look hopeful at him. It was taking attention from him, and putting it on Billy's unexpected good news!

There would be no coming back from this moment. Not only did he lie about not having his grades, he added a layer of falsehood. It was too late for them to call the school, and double check his story. If they called the school tomorrow, and started asking questions, it wouldn't matter anyway, because it would be too late.

"...I'm gone." Billy thought to himself as he steeled himself in the face of his step mother's scrutiny.

He had to rescue both himself, and his brother from the torment of the metal chair, and threat of beatings for poor grades. Billy knew his death from suicide would force the issue, and it would free him of it, and save his brother from the same treatment.

His step mother looked away, and for a brief moment, Billy smiled at his younger brother. They were seven years apart. Billy 16, and his brother only 9, they weren't close, but he loved him. They had separate mothers, but the same father, and it was Billy's mother's inherit nature that really triggered his father's rage at times.

Billy trained himself to read his father's subtle cues, and try and predict his mood, and triggers so he could minimize the danger to himself. He was certain he could almost predict his father's mood before he got home by the sound of his truck tires as they approached the house from a mile away. The truck tires were large, and if they sounded like they were racing towards the house, Billy anticipated his father would have a short fuse, and loaded for bear around the house.

If he were in one of those moods, he was more apt to throw things at Billy, cuss him like a rodent in the corn, or threaten to beat him with the heavy, belt-like strap. He watched his father's subtle cues like the barometric pressure as if he were trying to predict the weather, and if

Billy detected any variable that might suggest his father was in a volatile mood, he knew he had to do his best, and stay under the radar for the day. When he heard his father roll into the gravel driveway, Billy made a point to glance out a window, and watch, and listen. There were some nights when he came home in a good mood, perhaps jovial, and on those nights, Bill was granted a reprieve. He knew he could go to bed, and feel reasonably secure for the rest of the night, but only to do it all over the next day.

On this particular Thursday night, the kitchen ticked off time as Billy stood like a deer-in-the-headlight as he tried to convince his step mother of a grand deception. Lying was something that would certainly provoke the worst of his father's retribution, even the slightest fib was generally unwise. He wasn't lying to deflect an uncomfortable truth, he was scheming another reality, with the intention of hiding his drastic intentions. His father would be home soon, and it was very important for them to accept this story Billy was telling them.

"...uh yes, there was a glitch at school today, and though I generally struggle to pass each semester, this semester I passed with flying colors, and exceeded your expectations!"

If his father didn't believe him, and found the report cards in his pocket, he would hurt Billy. His step mother's warnings were generally grounded in fact. She knew the man could potentially hurt Billy. He had in the past, and so there was reason to suspect it would happen again.

Billy stood resolute. He took a beating once before, because he wasn't going to remain locked in a chair, and he wasn't going to continue to live under the threat of this man's menacing nature anymore.

The three of them heard the back door open, and slam shut as Billy's father came into the house. He couldn't see his father, but he could feel his energy across the small hair on his arms, and neck. He could feel the heaviness in the home like a barometer can measure the atmospheric pressure.

"...what's wrong with him?" The man asked Billy's step-mother.

Billy watched his stepmother defend her son. It appeared in slow motion, as Billy became dissociative, and watched the dynamic from what felt like a million miles away.

The man looked at Billy, unphased about his younger son's end of the semester report cards, and waited for Billy to speak up.

Now was the time to sell the lie, and make the same decision like he did when he decided to accept his father's beatings, over confinement. Billy knew it would all be over in less than twenty four hours. He had it planned. He was always at risk for suicide, especially once he started planning it, and now a crisis was pushing him over the cliff. He planned where, and how. It was never an easy proposition, but right now, it brought him peace, knowing soon his suffering would be a forgotten memory. Billy believed that once he pressed the trigger to a firearm, he would just wake up in the clouds, and find himself among Angels in heaven. No more suffering...

However, he really wasn't prepared for the reality of it. There was no way of fully knowing how he would respond to the approaching, self inflicted tragedy. Billy would have no way of knowing how his perspective would soon change, and that altered perspective would cause him to fully regret this moment.

His father often promised him, *"...I'll either make you, or break you boy."*

His father would regret those words when he saw his son's shattered body in the trauma room the next day.

Standing in front of his old locker much like he'd done over twenty years ago, Bill could remember those words that his father spoke to him so often.

He could also remember the conversation he had with himself as he stood in front of his locker, an hour before shooting himself in the woods behind his home.

"...would it hurt?"

"...will it be over quickly?"

"...am I ready?"

The hallway was empty right now, but twenty plus years ago, on that Friday, the halls were full of vivacious, loud teenagers, excited it was Friday!

"...would any of them notice I was gone on Monday?"

"...why didn't anyone see?"

"...why me, and not someone else?"

Bill remembered feeling the longing. The longing to feel safe. Longing to live his life like his peers. Longing to feel loved at home. Nurtured. He remembered Billy was exhausted, and could no longer waste away in the chair, locked away, because of a slight. He was a good kid. His teachers liked him. He never got in any real trouble, and certainly never did any drugs like some of those other kids, who seemed to find trouble. Billy read the Bible, sometimes. He remembered praying often to God, and asking Him to make his father stop hurting him, but the bad things never seemed to stop.

Bill remembered the questions Billy had, but standing today, he knew the answers to many of those questions.

Bill walked back towards Erika. He followed the same route that led him out of the school on that Friday afternoon as he headed to the waiting school bus. He saw the ghost-like apparitions of many teachers and waved *"Happy Friday!"* and reminded students, *"Have a Safe Weekend!"*

Billy would be dead in a few hours, and none of them knew. Bill knew the loneliest walk anyone can take, is the last few hundred steps a person can make as they prepare themselves to end their life. The world goes on, and on, often unaware of the solitude of the individual who is planning on never seeing another sunrise.

Billy walked out of the school, empty handed, no books, no notebooks, or papers.

No one saw him.

No one wished him, "Happy Friday."

He felt intentional about what was going to happen next—he would not be here come Monday morning.

Bill found Erika and sat quietly beside her. Outside the wind blew, and snow fell, but next to Erika, Bill felt warm, and safe. He felt a reprieve from the untethered feeling of the flashbacks, and triggers of the night. He no longer laid in his bed at night, afraid someone was going to drag him from his bed in a fit of rage, and demand that he go back out into the rainy night, and finish his chore list. Erika, and his kids lived in a peaceful home, unmarred by any domestic violence, they struggled financially everyday, and the rat race of trying to keep up wore Bill down. He felt his father's harsh, critical words everyday as he measured himself against whatever perceived expectation the man put over Billy as he grew into an adult.

Bill forgot his gift.

Sitting now, overwhelmed by the demands of the rat race, troubled by the ghosts of flashbacks, and triggers, Bill remembered the gift Billy was given.

How could he forget he thought to himself?

It was a pivotal realization about life...

Maybe it was survivors' guilt, because few people survived what Billy did, and Bill felt obligated to measure his life's success on the vague notion of "The American Dream."

Maybe he felt he had to prove to his father, and make an account of himself out of respect for those who were successful in their suicide. He remembered the regret, it was the regret that changed his perspective that night after he discharged a firearm at himself. He fought like hell to survive after firing the weapon, but a miracle saved his life, but so many people are lost, and surely they also felt the same regret Billy did.

"Are you okay?" Erika asked.

"Yeah, I'm fine, but I would like to leave in a couple of hours."

"Sure, we can go whenever you're ready. I can tell you're having a hard time," she said, as she reassured him, and tried to comfort him.

Chapter Six

"Before we leave tonight, I would like one dance with you," Erika asked, leaning into Bill with a warm, nurturing smile.

He needed that.

Bill smiled, and nodded his head with a grin.

Things felt normal for a moment. He was grounded, a brief respite from the onslaught of flashbacks, and painful, traumatic memories.

"That's a great idea...I would love that."

Sliding their chairs out, and walking hand-in-hand towards the makeshift dance floor, Bill slid his arm around Erika's waist, and began to slowly move in rhythm to a One-Hit-Wonder of a bygone decade.

Bill smelled the familiar smell of Erika's conditioner, and shampoo, and it was reassuring, and an everyday fixture of the present. He could see the way the shimmering, cascading light, reflecting off a cheesy disco ball added to the understanding today, was today. He was safe, not another decade, years ago. Bill felt safe, and empowered holding the woman he loved, and cared for. Their children would never live cowering in their beds, and endure the hellish suffering of an ugly, brown metal, folding chair, or endure the humiliation of plates of food thrown at them, because a parent lost control.

Despite the security he felt in the moment, he was still standing over the same ground he once walked towards what he felt was his final, resolute moment. That ground served as an energy reservoir, a bank, ready to channel that remaining kinetic energy back into Bill, because of the trauma Billy suffered. The damning, critical words his father used to carve up his heart, and mind left wounds. The bullet scar pounded, and tore at his vulnerable skin as the aspirin he took many hours ago wore off, leaving him to suffer the familiar aches, and pains. As the dance went on, Bill's scars were hidden, and unseen to everyone else.

He felt weak, vulnerable, broken as the scars screamed, and shouted at him. He didn't feel normal, compared to everyone else. These grounds held terrible memories of something he almost didn't survive. Something he tried to hide, and pretend never happened.

"...what does she see in me?" Bill thought to himself as Erika rested her head on his shoulder.

Those words his father used to carve his heart, and self worth were condemning him.

The sun from another era pierced the night above Bill as he danced with Erika beneath a snowy night.

The sunlit memory from another time felt like a flat carbonated drink that's lost its sparkling bubble. He saw the cheerleaders flip, and bounce among dinner tables as alumni went on with their night, unaware their younger doppelgangers were chasing becoming the older version of themselves as they wished their lives away for another weekend. Bill knew Billy wanted to live his life like his friends, and classmates. He was tired of having his father screaming in his face, and threatening him in one, or another, most days of his life. He didn't want to commit suicide, but he was broken, exhausted after years of life inside of a prison camp, and suicide seemed to offer his only hope of escape from the prison's walls.

Billy would often wonder if the other kids panicked when they heard their father come home?

Did they live day to day in survival mode?

Did they try to predict their father's moods, and subsequent potential harms?

What was it like to live in a safe house?

Billy knew it was pointless to ask these questions, because this was his lot in life. It was his lip that was left bloodied, and swollen, because he *"pissed"* his father off. His back hurt, because he'd been sitting restrained for twelve hours on a Saturday. Billy walked out of that school on that faded, sunlit day at 3:15 PM intent on exchanging his life for what he imagined was liberation, and freedom from all of those things.

Bill held Erika tightly as they moved in sync to the rhythm of the sound of the music playing. Her warm breathing was a fraying tether to the safety of the present, anchoring Bill on the shores of today, despite the storm of yesterday's trauma. The post traumatic stress of the survived trauma, and what he had to do to survive had a grip on both his mind, and body.

Erika whispered she loved Bill as he felt the grip on reality grow dark, and the power of the past illuminated his emotions, and senses. Time, and space simply blended together as the stored energy in the building opened one last time capsule for Bill to relive, and see the thing he so desperately wanted to avoid.

Billy boarded the noisy school bus for the final time as the bus started to rumble towards his destination. **Home.** He was exhausted, and needed a nap on the way home. On most days the drive home took a little over an hour. The last thing Billy wanted to do was count the stops the bus made, and watch the miles slide past as the wheels carried him towards the end. The world went on around him, oblivious to what his intentions were.

The bus stopped in front of his home, and let Billy off without incident. The bus was on time, and there was no reason for any suspicion that anything was wrong. The only people at home during this time of day were his little brother, and grandfather. He only had two hours to follow through on what took him many months to plan. There was no time to stop, and reflect, or back out, because he would have to face his father's rage on Monday. This was the only window in time for him to see this all the way through. His grandfather wasn't paying attention, and his little brother was simply preoccupied.

Both of his parents would be home in a couple of hours, and remain home all weekend. No, there was no time to pause this. He painted himself into a corner of desperation as he waved at the busdriver, and watched her drive away in a cloud of exhaust.

He was alone in the street.

Billy went inside the house and passed his grandfather as he took a nap on the couch. The TV in the living room was on, and it made it easier for Billy to do what he had to do. He saw his brother watching TV in another room, and paid no attention to Billy. He understood, because Billy never gave anyone reason to believe he was about to do something so rash, and drastically traumatic. The consequences of this would be something, Billy would not be able to undo. His parents, teachers, and few friends never anticipated this either. There were clues, symptoms, but if anyone noticed, no one intervened, and asked him, "Do you need help?"

He entered his bedroom and closed the door behind him. He went to his desk, sat down, and took out a piece of paper, and started writing. Billy felt obliged to say something. Billy didn't really want to take his life. What he *really* wanted to do was go to the basketball game at school, and hang out with the other kids at someone's house later, and watch movies. However, this was his only chance to escape the walls of what felt like a prison for many years. In another time, and place, and perhaps in another universe he liked to believe he was living a happy life. His mouth suddenly felt dry as crackers, and he desperately needed a sip of water.

Billy left his bedroom and walked past his brother. He felt sad, and he wanted to spare him as much as possible from this terrible thing he was about to do, but he remembered the fear he saw in his face last night. Billy had to change things, and it seemed the only way. He went into the bathroom, closed the door, and turned on the faucet. As he let the water flow over his hands, he felt that familiar feeling of dissociation. He looked at his face in the mirror, felt the water flowing over his hands, but none of it felt real. It felt very dreamlike. His eyes were now hollow, lifeless, sunken deep as if they were already acquainted with how death might look once he stepped out in front of it. He rinsed his mouth out, spit, and went and got his coat from the closet.

This was the moment in his plan where he felt he was at the greatest risk for discovery. Once he removed the rifle from the unlocked gun cabinet and hid it in his coat, there was no turning back if his grandfather woke up, and saw him. It was also Friday, and because of that, he ran the small risk his father *might* come home early, and this would go very bad if he found him.

Billy went into his father's study where he kept his collection of many guns. He opened the unlocked gun cabinet, and removed a small .22 caliber rifle. It was small, and something he could smuggle in his coat, and ultimately out of the house. It was also symbolic, because it was his gun. His father bought it for him as a Christmas present, but Billy never wanted a gun. He liked toys, bikes, games, anything but guns, and knives. His father was always trying to make him into something Billy never wanted to be.

At the top of the gun cabinet Billy found boxes of bullets. He removed one bullet from the box, and put it in his pocket. He wrapped the rifle in his coat, held his breath, and stepped out in plain view in front of his sleeping grandfather. If he were going to get caught, now would be that moment.

He breathed a momentary sigh of relief, his grandfather never stirred.

He was still napping.

As the TV blared on—Billy crept past, unaware of the events happening just feet away from him. Billy walked past his brother, he remained engrossed in the TV, and also unaware of the rifle rolled up inside of Billy's winter coat.

Back in his bedroom, Billy sighed with relief. He successfully retrieved the gun from his father's gun cabinet without drawing attention to himself, and risked his plan coming apart. There was no turning back at this point. Looking out his bedroom window, Billy realized there was still risk of detection, because once he climbed out of his bedroom window, he would have to run a half a mile towards the woods. Once he was tucked inside of the woods, and out of sight, he would be alone with his intentions, and finally be free of this. One hundred yards from the edge of the woods, Billy knew there was a small creek that meandered through his parent's property, and it afforded the ideal, peaceful spot to finish what he planned to do.

It was also far enough away that the sound of the shot would draw little, if any attention, because it was hunting season, and not uncommon to hear the sound of occasional gun fire from a hunter's gun. There was a small farm lane that ran adjacent to Billy's parent's property, and several dozen steps away from his bedroom window. This farm lane would help conceal his escape, and help him remain out of sight as he ran in the direction of the woods with the firearm.

Billy folded his suicide note in half, and slid it into his final report cards, and folded them all together, and put them into his breast pocket. He had changed his shirt, and decided to wear a shirt, and tie at the last minute.

"...I want to look decent when they find me."

Billy also saw his small Bible resting on a shelf next to his bedroom window, and decided to take it with him. He planned everything, but the Bible was a last minute course correction in his suicide planning. If he read a passage, or two of scripture, would he find some peace, or comfort during these final moments? Would it be enough to find inspiration, and or guidance? Perhaps a more hopeful resolution, and alternative to suicide if he read some divinely inspired scripture right now? Billy didn't have the answers to these questions, but it was comforting to have the Bible on him; so he slid it into his pocket at the last minute.

He slid his bedroom window open, and carefully slid the rifle out of the window, propping it up against the side of the house. He listened for a moment. Quiet.

"...Goodbye."

Billy climbed out of the bedroom window, and landed softly next to the rifle. He felt alarmed, panicked, because if he were discovered right now, there would be no explaining any of this.

Shirt, and tie. Slacks. Rifle. Bible. Report Cards. Suicide Note...

"...what the hell are you doing boy?" That's how that conversation would begin if anyone found him.

It was now, or never, and he needed to run towards the woods.

Billy grabbed the rifle, and started to run towards the dirt road that would lead him in the direction of the woods.

"...No going back."

His heart was racing as he ran the race to end his life. He felt as if he were escaping a prison, as he jumped the prison walls, and soon felt the Warden would send the hounds after him as soon as they discovered Billy escaped their custody.

Though he felt his body race with adrenalin, he felt sadness, because he missed school. He missed his friends, and the kids he went to school with. He wished he was at the Basketball game more than anything. He wished he had been normal, and loved. That life was out of his reach.

Billy reached the end of the dirt road. The small farm lane hid his escape from discovery. He felt relieved no one saw him running towards the woods with the firearm. Billy was more afraid of the consequences of discovery than the drastic measures he was moments away from.

Once he felt secure, tucked away in the woods, and free from discovery he walked one hundred steps towards the direction of the little creek he once played in during hot summer days. It was a peaceful spot.

Billy saw a discarded, green plastic crate lying next to a tree. It was discarded, and forgotten by his father, perhaps used to tote odd tools around as he worked in the woods, cutting firewood. It would make an ideal stool for him to sit down on as he loaded the firearm, read some scripture, and prepared himself. He flipped the green, plastic crate over, and sat down gently, placing the rifle across his lap. He looked at his watch, and noted the time. It was a little after four, and his father would be home before six.

This had to be over no later than five...

His father could not discover him in this position, especially with a pocket full of bad report cards. Report cards he lied about, and how would he explain away the rifle?

A suicide note?

It had to be over right now!

Billy heard the sound of the bubbling creek as the water flowed over the pebble rock bed, as it twisted, and meandered through the woods around him.

He could hear the gentle sound of an inherent breeze rustling the brown, dead winter leaves in the treetops above. He felt cold. Swallowing his dry spit, Billy realized this was the loneliest place for anyone to find themselves in. He remembered playing in the creek on hazy, humid summer days in what now felt like another lifetime.

Billy rested his back against the tree, and suddenly felt chilled to the bone. He didn't realize he was soaking wet from sweat. His legs felt cold, and he could hear his teeth chattering.

He was scared.

He watched his breath float up towards the cold, early evening winter sky.

"...Friday, January 24." He said.

He felt it was important to recognize the date.

The rifle felt heavy in his lap, and he could actually smell it. It smelled like metal, gun oil, and brass. It felt smooth in his hands. He felt nauseated. He didn't dress warm for this, and the lightweight slacks provided little warmth against the January air. The thin slacks also offered very little cushion for the rifle resting in his lap, and the weight of the weapon felt like a mountain crushing him underneath.

The shivering hurt his bones, and teeth.

Other than the sound of the steady breeze, and bubbling creek, the woods were as still as a cemetery. It was the proverbial calm before the storm.

Billy missed the sound of the chaos life brings. He missed the feeling of the warm sun on his face, and he realized he would never feel that again. He hated the smell of the rifle, and the smell of the woods, and the smell of winter.

He was trying to ignore the alarm bells. He was already doubting. Hesitating.

Without realizing it, Billy discovered at least one reason to *live...he missed the warmth of the sunshine.* He hated the smell of winter. Felt like he was sitting in a cemetery inside of the isolation of the woods. The woods grew dark as the sun started to sink behind the small mountain ridge a few miles away. The shadows growing across the forest floor heralded the lateness of the moment, and time was getting away from him.

Eventually he would have to swallow, remove the safety, and end it.

This had to be over soon, because Monday would be here no matter what, and his father was expecting a stellar report card, not the drek he had in his shirt pocket.

His breathing was rapid, and shallow. Sweat was now beading over his brow, and his butt ached from the uncomfortable, cold plastic crate.

He thought of his friends, classmates at school right now, and wished one last time he was living like them. Billy also wished he had thought to dress warmer.

A hat.

Perhaps some gloves.

He never anticipated how impossible this moment would feel. He never imagined that he would hesitate, costing him time. Time he did not have. Billy had planned—that by now he would be dead.

But "*dead*" was permanent.

He was standing on the precipice, flinching. Hesitating.

He remembered the Bible, and pulled it out from his coat pocket, and opened it. The wind blew, and flipped the pages as he stared at the printed words on the page.

"...Leviticus."

"...Exodus."

"...Job."

He tried to read some scriptures. It was written in King James, and the words were blurry, and didn't resonate with him. With his back against the tree, and a gun resting in his lap, Billy slowly turned the pages as he searched for an answer. He wasn't sure what that answer would look like if he saw it, but he knew if there were one, he would recognize it.

He tossed the Bible to the ground. The trees would all be witness to his final moments. Billy's will-to-live was suddenly aroused, and understood this was no fantasy of escapism, or a "cry for help." He intended to use this gun on himself, and his *fight-or-flight* was trying to reason with him, and go back home. He was afraid to die. The roar of this desperate internal struggle of life, and death was exhausting.

He believed a sincere prayer would be the right thing to do right now, and perhaps God would respond this one time when Billy felt he desperately needed God's help.

"Dear God, please send an angel to save me. Amen."

Before Billy opened his eyes after saying, "Amen" he sincerely believed God heard him, and this time he would see an angelic member of the Heavenly Host standing among the trees, but to his disappointment...there was nothing, but the dead, winter brown as far as his eyes could see as he glanced around the woods.

"...You see, even God does not see, or care about you. Now shoot!"

Billy heard that savage, mockingly critical voice demand that he follow through on his suicide plan, and shoot himself. He heard this voice with such clarity. It felt as if there was someone standing directly behind him, and looking over his shoulder in pathetic disgust.

The strain was too much, and without realizing it, he drifted off to sleep.

He was not sure how long he was asleep when he abruptly woke up, and glanced at his watch. It was now 5 P.M. and he was out of time. He had lost the resolve to take his life. His head throbbed, and his mouth felt so dry. He wanted to run away from the corner he had painted himself into, and run somewhere safe, but he was trapped. His mind was clawing him away from this moment, and the brief nap seemed to edge him back away from the ledge of the abyss. Billy was in a hard retreat, and pulling out of the nose dive as his will-to-live appeared to have won over the intentions of suicide.

"I can't do this!" He shouted as he jumped to his feet.

His feet felt heavy as he started to trudge home. He felt a tremendous sense of relief he had not gone through with it, and he needed to get back home, and return the rifle back to the gun cabinet before his father got home. Retracing his steps, the dead leaves crunched under the weight of his feet as he walked in the direction of home. The unused bullet was still in his pocket. His report cards, the ones he lied about the night before, were wrapped tightly by his suicide note. The Bible he hoped would shed some much needed light on this moment, resting on the ground by the plastic crate.

Billy stopped.

He couldn't go home.

He lied.

"...he'll hurt me."

Nothing scared him more.

There would be a reckoning.

"...why did I have to lie? Why did I have to tell him my report cards 'were actually good'? Because they weren't."

He knew what it felt like to be a helpless animal ensnared in a trap, unable to escape, unless he chewed off his own ankle. He was powerless to stop his father, and no one who had the ability to stop him was going to step in, and intervene on his, and his brother's behalf. He could not escape the gravity of his father's abuses, and it was pulling him towards the ledge of self-destruction in desperation. It was a dead end. Like an exhausted swimmer caught within a deadly rip current pulling him away from the safety of dry ground the undertow of despair carried him back to the tree, and green plastic crate.

Billy sat down.

Opened the rifle's bolt action.

He pulled the bullet from his pocket, and dropped the bullet into the rifle.

He closed the bolt action.

Billy slid the gun's safety off so the gun was ready to fire.

He pivoted the loaded firearm so it was pointing at him.

He watched his breath float upwards towards the treetops. He would soon be free of this suffering like the air he exhaled. He felt the weight of the gun barrel resting on his chest. He worried this might hurt, but he told himself he would probably never remember how it felt, because he would wake up in heaven moments later.

"...There was no reason to fear," he told himself.

He was going to fly like he once did on his bicycle during happier moments in his life. Though he had to traverse this moment, there was hope on the other side he told himself.

He focused on one point in the grey, winter sky, and tried to block out the sight of the loaded gun barrel as it menaced him.

Billy reached down the length of the rifle, and felt the trigger with his thumb as he continued to gaze skyward.

He heard the creek's water flow not far away. The trigger felt cold to touch.

He pushed the trigger with right thumb.

The rifle fired.

Billy was never the same.

He had fired this same gun before with his father, but he never remembered it sounding this loud as the gun fired inches below his face. A camera flashbulb like light scarred his sense of sight, and memory as the roar of the shot reverberated through both him, and the woods.

"Oh Jesus," Billy moaned, and gasped as he rolled off the plastic crate. His body collapsed to the ground like dead weight. He felt like a Major League Baseball player just slammed him in the chest with a molten hot, iron poker, taken from a searing fire as an unbearable feeling of heat tore him apart as the bullet did what it was designed to do.

Nothing could have prepared him for this.

Billy was not in heaven. He was not flying like he felt when he rode his bike.

There was nothing freeing about this. There wasn't anything romantic about this, because those suicidal ideations deceived him into believing this was a legitimate option when he strongly considered, and planned to take his life.

He was gasping to breathe on the cold ground.

Gradually the ringing in his ears subsided, and once more he could hear the sound of the bubbling creek not far away.

He was surprised he was still alive.

He felt as if he'd been hit by a truck sized object, and there was going to be a hole the size of a basketball in the middle of him.

Afraid to look down at the hole in him, Billy kept his gaze skyward, and listened to the bubbling creek.

"*...why am I still alive?*"

He had to look down, but he was scared to see what he might see.

"*...that hole is going to be so enormous,*" he thought as he continued to gasp for his next breath.

His body felt broken. Different. Weirdly shattered, snapped in half. He glanced down. Billy was shocked to see only a small tear in his light blue parka.

A single, white feather protruded from the small tear in his parka.

One delicate feather.

He was confused, and in shock. Billy felt the world explode into him when he fired the rifle at himself, but in spite of that nightmarish heat, and explosive energy, he was alive, and what he saw was a single, lazy feather in the small tear in his coat.

Billy suddenly felt a hot, sticky sensation lurking just under his coat, and shirt.

Whatever was leaking, it was leaking fast.

Billy smelled a sweet smell, a smell he would never forget, because it's the smell of something very specific.

He unzipped his parka just a little, and saw that his shirt was soaking wet. He felt as if he were drowning on dry ground with each inspiration he made as he struggled to breathe.

He wanted to sit up so he could breathe, but his body felt noncompliant. It felt shattered, broken, and he didn't feel in control of it.

He regretted pushing the trigger. He wanted his life back the way it was just before pushing the trigger. Yes he was afraid of his father, and suffered for many years, but this was so much worse than anything his father could do.

"*...I would take a thousand reasons why I just shot myself, if I could have my life back right now.*"

His grey shirt was drenched from hemorrhaging. His suicide note, and report cards were now stained in blood.

Things were bad, but they were going to get much worse. Billy felt terrible regret for shooting himself. He wanted his life back. He wanted it back, but it was too late. He was going to die, and he didn't want that. He regretted he would never see another day of sunshine.

Billy heard someone speak to him.

He heard a distinct voice.

The voice was very still, calming.

This disembodied voice knew him, but Billy didn't know who was speaking to him.

This voice was not the sound of his own thoughts, because this voice was calm despite Billy's tormented thoughts, and racing mind. Billy was an adolescent, but this voice was mature, wise, and commanded an air of authority. It was unmoved, unwavering, and calming to Billy's fears, and suffering. It seemed to whisper from both within Billy, but also sounded as if it came from just feet away as the stranger watched, ready to lend a helping hand.

"Name a reason to live," the calm voice asked.

Someone was speaking to Billy, even if he couldn't see them, and despite the dire nature of the moment, he felt it was important to offer an answer to the important question.

The unseen, invisible speaker was waiting patiently for Billy's response.

He felt as if he were drowning, and his breathing was deteriorating by the minute.

He was afraid to die alone, and he wanted his life back desperately. But that moment had come, and gone.

This was the reality of suicide.

Forever.

He wanted to live.

Billy heard the distinct sound of children laughing, giggling, playing. It felt like a life affirming sound, but he didn't recognize who these children were. These weren't his memories, but though he wasn't familiar with these children, he felt an undeniable connection to them.

The laughter, and energy felt rambunctious, full of life, as he felt hope for a future, though he had never experienced any of this in his own home. It didn't matter he was at the present moment, dying in the woods, he felt hope. He could look past this present suffering, and find one reason to hope in.

Though he'd never heard any one of these children on a playground, or park, they felt familiar as he embraced that connection. The once isolation of the woods became a beaming, vibrant place of hope, and love as Billy felt peace, joy, and love. These children weren't ghosts from the past, but a promise of the future if he would pivot his life away from this place, and fight for his life! His perspective was changing, and he found a reason to live. He believed he was given a glimpse into the future, an eyewitness of what might become, if he fought for his life.

He tried to imagine what their faces looked like, because he knew this was a wrinkle in time. His life wasn't flashing back, but rather flashing forward, if he survived. He felt the power of hope fight back against the ravages of despair!

He knew in this wrinkle of time, Billy was sharing an ice cream cone with these children, and they were acting silly in a childlike manner. It felt like a glitch in time, and he was suddenly privy to knowing a group of children he'd never met before.

Acquainted, and familiar with them....

Time had somehow bent, folded back on him in this narrow space between life, and imminent death. His life flash forward gave him hope, and a reason to want to live! Billy didn't feel alone. Forgotten.

Billy might not feel love at home, but one day, he could provide a loving home of his own. He might not feel love, but he could give love to someone else.

He had an answer to the disembodied stranger who asked him a question.

Billy wanted to be a dad.

He may die now, but at least he would die fighting for his life.

He can't un-ring a bell, or bring the bullet back, but he would move far away from this place, and move towards life.

"I want to be a dad," Billy stated.

"That's a good reason. Crawl now," his guide directed.

The sound of children playing went quiet, still, but they were never forgotten. Billy pulled his strength together, as he started his fight to live. He rolled over, and fought to get back up on his feet. The sensation of drowning made moving near impossible.

He had to get to his feet!

Billy found the strength to stand, and tried to ignore the sense the ground was heaving under his feet as he took his first steps towards help. He was going to have to retrace his steps, and it was a long walk back to his house, because he had gone out of his way to die. Billy had to overcome his best laid plans. He had regrets. *He never anticipated he would actually regret taking his life, and want to undo this suicide!!!*

It never, not once entered his thinking that once he pulled the trigger to a firearm that was aimed at himself, or any other lethal means of suicide, he might wished like hell, he hadn't. He had to walk almost a half a mile to find help, but that was only the beginning, because the nearest hospital was at least twenty miles away. He was weak, unable to breathe, and getting weaker by the minute from the loss of blood.

He wanted to live!

He lowered his shoulders like a football player, and tried to lumber, and crash his way forward through the unforgiving woods as if he were breaking tackles on a football field. Without warning one of his legs gave out, and he fell face first into the side of a tree. Billy saw blinding stars, but the pain barely registered. There was no time to lay there, and just appreciate he had just smashed his face into the side of a tree! In another time, and place, that blow to his face would have been a substantial moment, but he was engaged in a savage fight to survive. He had to stand back up, and keep moving forward at all costs.

He used the tree to get back on his feet. He felt as if he were suddenly blind out of one eye, and unable to see anymore after smashing his face against the tree.

He had to move on...

Fight to live...

There was no stopping...

Survival...

This is the only thing that matters...

His will to live was calling the shots, and calling audibles as it tried to survive his best inetended suicide plan.

The ground once more pitched, and heaved as if he were on the deck of a ship lost within a howling storm. Trying in vain, the ground felt spongy, and unpredictable to him as he struggled to walk the distance towards salvation.

He fell hard once more to the ground, but it barely registered.

"...I don't want to die," he heard himself say.

This was real. This was now his reality, if he didn't get to help soon, he was going to die from suicide, and die with regrets.

His legs, and feet would not cooperate with him, and support his weight. Lying on the ground it felt as if a fully grown man were standing on his back. It was impossible.

Billy was in dire straits, but not alone.

Once more the voice of the disembodied voice spoke to him.

"Crawl!" the unseen stranger commanded.

The unseen voice was acting as a guide, coaching Billy towards possible rescue. There was no time to question if this voice belonged to an unseen Angel, or if the voice was just a figment of Billy's desperate attempt at survival. The source of the voice appeared to have an understanding of what it would take for him to survive, and if Billy did as instructed, the source of the voice remained assured he would survive. The source of the voice was invested, committed to helping Billy.

Every tree, every log, every sharp rock presented an obstacle to rescue as he started crawling for his life. What crawling did was afford a more stable surface for him to move over. It was a solid surface to dig his arms, and feet into as he dragged himself through the rough terrain. His dragged his swollen, and bruised face over jagged saw briars, and rocks as he pulled himself with his arms, and pushed with his feet. His lungs worked with a diminished, fevered capacity, but unwilling to give up without a fight.

He was getting weaker, but despite this, he felt his body surge forward across the frozen earth, as if unseen hands were dragging him. Helping him. A rescue by Angels. His legs felt limp, useless, but he was moving forcefully across the jagged earth. Billy felt as if his face were nearly bouncing off the ground as if he were being dragged by a team of sled dogs.

He didn't remember the moment when he broke free from the isolation of the saw briars, and the unforgiving woods, and found himself lying in a field several hundred yards behind his house. Billy was closer to rescue, but still no one knew he was laying out of sight, a small bloody speck in an empty field no one would give a second glance towards.

He could move no more.

He rolled over onto his back and looked up in distress at the gray, winter sky. He was not safe yet, but he was relieved he was no longer laying in the woods. If he were going to die, he was going to die right here, but at least they would know he died trying to save himself from this regrettable decision.

He didn't want to die alone.

Why didn't he consider any of this?

Billy glanced down at himself, and he realized his shoes were gone. His once light blue parka was in tatters, and soaking wet. It was full of twigs, and broken sticks. It was smeared with green moss, dirt, and saturated with his blood. His ragged parka told the story of his desperate attempt at surviving the ravages of suicide. Lying on his back, and with nothing but sky to look at Billy felt as if he were falling up into the sky. A leaf, untethered from a branch, swept away by the force of wind as it flies effortlessly from its tethered place in life. No longer feeling tethered inside of his body, and unsure if he were dead, or alive, Billy planted his gaze at a single treetop, hoping the reference point would help anchor him.

Time was running out.

"Call for help," the stranger directed him again.

Billy was grateful to hear the voice again.

A friend.

A compassionate friend during a dark, and terrible hour of his life.

Billy felt as if he were surviving on gulps of air at this point. The hoovering stranger, whispered, directed Billy to cry out for help.

How?

He could barely breathe, barely whisper. Now if he wanted to survive, he had to find the reserves from within himself to shout out loud, and scream for help.

Who?

Who would hear him?

He was reminded as he shook uncontrollably from shock—he actually planned this. It was all in his downward suicide spiral. The near convulsing made him feel as if he were going to snap in half from the force of his bones jarring, shaking.

The reasons he just shot himself felt forgotten, insignificant, and paled in comparison to this suffering, and hell. Billy never felt relief for pulling the trigger to the firearm he purposely aimed at himself. He regretted this.

He felt...anger.

Suicide stole the liberty of living from him. There was liberty in making decisions. There was liberty in the hope a new sunrise brings with it each day. Billy learned life was a gift, because each day brings new hope, new decisions, and a fresh perspective can offer a new hope for the new day. Suicide had burned down all of his chances for a new day, and a new perspective for life. He was watching himself die, and he felt as if he'd been duped into a cunning, deceptive thought that urged him to sign away all of his tomorrows. There will be no more tomorrow. He could no longer feel why he decided to take his life, because all he felt right now was grief, regret, and death. The glimmer of living was slipping away in the rear view mirror, and he wasn't ready.

Billy could blame no one, not even his father, because he was paying the price, and blaming someone wasn't going to help him. He had to find the strength to yell with the voice of a hundred men if he wanted to see another sunrise! He knew God heard him, and he knew there were Angels visiting him. God did answer Billy's prayer, and sent an Angel to intervene.

"Help!" He shouted. Trusting the word was carried on the wings of an Angel.

He coughed and cried again.

Silence.

He turned his thoughts to happy things. Things he would do tonight if he were a dad to those children he heard in the woods. They would build forts, play with trucks, and trains. They would watch silly shows on TV, and wrestle, and laugh until their stomachs hurt. Billy would read stories, and tell them he loved them. They would go to bed safe, and never lay awake in fear their father would drag them from their bed and hit, or yell at them.

Hope is a powerful engine.

Hope can overcome the impossible.

Hope wasn't predicated on Billy's circumstances, because hope was a change in perspective, and once that was put into motion, it became a moving life force.

...Things could get better.

Billy let go of the anchoring tree as he turned his eyes back up at the sky, and with the last bit of strength he yelled, and with the force of a roaring Lion he heard his voice soar far into the sky...

"For God's sake, please help me!"

He was feeling lighter than air. Something inside of him was starting to shift, and detach from himself. Billy felt as if his physical body were a tent, and the tent poles were getting pulled out, and he would soon move on from this earth.

No one was coming. He was dying. This was the reality of suicide.

"For God's sake please help!" He shouted one last time.

Billy sensed the earth was vibrating. The ground was shaking beneath his back. Footsteps. Someone was running towards him.

Billy rolled his head to the side, and saw his frightened brother. His brother's face was etched in shock, and fear. Billy was bad off, and though his brother was in shock, terrified, and immersed in this traumatic moment, Billy needed his help.

"Please get help. I've shot myself, and I don't want to die."

His brother's life changed forever when he saw Billy dying in that field on that cold, Friday, January night. He did not ask to be there at this moment, and he was afraid, numb from shock, but he responded to the moment with courage, and love as he raced off to get help.

There was nothing more Billy could do to try, and save himself except concentrate on breathing. The ground was rock hard, and unforgiving as he shook painfully. It had been less than one hour since he had taken the steps to end his life, but now he was desperately holding on to the fraying edges of life. He was afraid to close his eyes, uncertain he would ever open them again.

Billy heard the sound of more running footsteps. Turning his head, he saw his grandfather running towards him. In another time, and in another place, because of his pack a day smoking habit, watching his grandfather run was nothing short of a miraculous thing to see. He wanted to smile when he saw his grandfather. He was a strong man, a Second World War combat veteran, and his presence was comforting. There were Angels at work in many forms, intervening on Billy's behalf.

His grandfather knelt beside him and stroked his grandson's head, reassuring him that help was on the way, and he was not alone.

"I'm sorry," Billy whispered. He felt remorseful. The reasons why he shot himself were no longer important to him. These were the consequences of choosing suicide.

He cradled Billy's head in his lap, and sat quietly.

"The ambulance is coming," his grandfather promised.

Later Billy would learn...*his brother was relaxing in the warm house, and watching cartoons, when there was an urgent, and inexplicable need to go outside, and in the direction of the woods behind their house. Once outside, he was to gather firewood, and he was to, "GO NOW!" There wasn't even time to dress warmly, because when Billy saw his brother, he was dressed in only a t-shirt, and jeans. His brother felt the need to run out of the warm house, and into the cold winter weather, gather firewood, and by a miraculous intervention, saved his brother, because he found him in time. He heard Billy crying for help as he ran outside to go gather firewood.*

"I don't want to die," Billy cried. He wanted to see another sunrise. He was only sixteen, and as the moment was teaching him, had so much to live for.

"The ambulance will be here soon. I don't believe you're going to die today son. You have a light of fight left Billy, so please, keep fighting, and stay with me."

His grandfather took his coat off, and used it to cover Billy's shaking body.

Billy knew the ambulance was coming. It was a race against time. He didn't know how far the ambulance was or how long it would take to arrive. Every minute was an agonizing ordeal, as he desperately fought to survive something he planned for many months. He was soaking wet, but not from water. He could smell it. Sticky. Sweet. Smelled like, or tasted like Copper. It was draining out of him.

Blood.

So much of it.

The small, rural volunteer fire department was eight miles away.

During daytime hours the volunteers were summoned to the fire station from their jobs, farms, and homes, before they could respond to the scene of an emergency.

He would have to wait.

The ambulance, once on scene, would have a twenty minute transport time to the hospital.

Billy would have to keep fighting if he wanted to survive.

He started to doubt if he would see another sunrise, and he doubted he would live to become a dad, or share his love with others. He was starting to sputter like a car running on fumes as he lost consciousness, and drifted into a black hole, and felt nothing until he woke back up.

He awoke to the sight of uniformed men looking down at him. Two police officers were standing over him, and their expressions were grim, and alarming. They appeared to accept Billy would be dead soon, and they had to gather information before he passed. They had a job to do, and for them, this was just another day in the office, "*nothing personal son.*"

"Who shot you?" One of them asked.

Billy could no longer speak. He motioned at himself to indicate that he shot himself.

The officer nodded.

"Where is the gun son?"

Without lifting his head, Billy pointed in the direction of the woods.

The officers nodded at him, and walked away to go about their business of collecting the firearm, and any other evidence necessary that this was a suicide.

He was fighting something no one else could see. He was slipping away into another reality, and feverishly clawing back from. He could not see this place, but intuitively knew it was close at hand.

Once more he felt the ground vibrate under him as a heavy vehicle rolled up near him, and stopped. He could hear a loud, crackling radio transmission, smell a reassuring smell of engine exhaust, and hear the sound of slamming doors, and urgent voices shouting at one another.

The ambulance had arrived. EMS crews knelt beside Billy and began their assessment of him.

Once again Billy became aware of something within himself trying to detach from his physical body. There was another perspective, a different reality, and he knew he was balanced precariously in-between the two different spaces. He was desperately holding on. Though things had been bad, very bad at home, surrendering his life was a tragic loss he would not be able to overcome if he died right now. There were reasons to hope, live, and that's what matters now.

A man with a very large box sat down, and opened the box as he prepared an IV for Billy. Billy moaned as he felt under his back once more for a bullet exit wound.

"No! There isn't an exit wound!" He shouted at his crew.

Billy asked the man to promise him he would not die.

"No. I won't promise you that, but I will promise I'll try to save you," the Paramedic replied bluntly.

Billy missed his grandfather's reassuring words. His life was now in the hands of strangers. There was no time to reassure him, and saving him was going to become a traumatic, brutal reality for Billy.

He felt them shift his body onto a backboard, and then lift him up onto a stretcher. They hoisted him up into a warm ambulance, and slammed the doors shut. He was unaware he slipped once more back into the dark abyss of unconsciousness.

Billy saw light.

Exhausted, and not wanting to leave this peaceful place, he was reluctant to leave the light, and return to the brutal fight to save his body.

She was sitting next to him.

Billy thought she was beautiful. She was calm, and seemed indifferent to the frantic pace going on all around him. She smiled, and held his hand. Her hand was warm, soft, and comforting. She wore a blue sweatshirt, and her red hair was pulled back into a bun. Her face vibrant with freckles, and her eyes twinkled blue as they radiated with compassionate energy. She studied Billy's eyes.

The sound of the siren, and rocking motion of the ambulance, reassured Billy he was in the hands of people, committed to saving him. Strangers to Billy, but strangers who were engaged in the frantic work to undo the damage his suicide attempt caused.

The pretty woman's voice sounded very far away to Billy as she spoke with him. He was teetering on the edge of an abyss the strangers in the Ambulance could not see. She was asking him questions about school. She asked Billy if he knew her daughter, because apparently they went to the same school. Billy felt it was a pretty random question given the nature of the present circumstances, but it was oddly comforting, because it was a normal, sane conversation, and it grounded him. He forgot for a brief moment, he was teetering on the precipice of life, and death.

He shook his head, "No."

He tried to place her, but he couldn't.

A totally polite, calm, normal conversation.

"Oh well, perhaps when you go back to school, you can look for her," she said as she continued to smile.

She stroked his hair, and seemed to just know, *"...you're going to make it."*

She seemed to speak words, without speaking them, but he was in shock, and he felt as if he were seeing things that might not be there.

She could be the one who was speaking with him in the woods, but maybe she was indeed a very kind, compassionate mom who volunteered to help that day save him. There were Angels surrounding him.

She blotted his eyes with a soft cotton gauze. He couldn't see out of one of his eyes, because of the fall against the tree. She encouraged him to take each breath. Despite all of the other hands working to stabilize him around a very crowded ambulance, she sat unphased, and calmly over her charge.

Once more he woke up from darkness, but she was still sitting next to him. She never seemed to move. The kind, pretty stranger just encouraged him to take his next breath, and gently wipe his eyes.

"Hi Billy," she said, "Welcome back. You're still with us. The ambulance will be at the hospital in a few minutes."

Despite the cramped commotion in the Ambulance, it always felt as if it was only the two of them in the back of the Ambulance as it raced to the hospital. He could hear other voices, and feel other hands working on his body . In an effort to keep him alive, she never broke his gaze. Her eyes never left his, and she never appeared to acknowledge the other members of the EMS crews. She wouldn't let him go, and kept him tethered to this side of life as she spoke softly, or blotted his face with gauze. There was an unbearable pressure on his chest that made him want to surrender, and let go, but she wouldn't let him. He couldn't breathe anymore, and he wanted to sleep. His body was shattered, done, and if these indeed were his final minutes he would be grateful he died next to this kind stranger. He would die with his dignity, and knowing he fought.

"...*Hard to breathe,*" he whispered.

"I know sweetheart, but I need you to keep trying for me. Focus on breathing. I promise you I can almost see the hospital, and you've come so far, you're going to make it."

He nodded his head.

Took another breath...

One more...

Another...

Focused...

An uphill battle...

Labored...

Gasp...

The backdoors of the Ambulance flew open as the EMS crews removed the stretcher with Billy's almost lifeless body.

She was gone.

No more painful breathing.

Darkness.

Rest.

Stillness.

Chapter Seven

An explosion of movement, and cold air dragged Billy back from the darkness, and back to the brutal suffering of enduring the fight to save his life. A large door whisked open, followed by the bitter, astringent smell of antiseptics, and bright intrusive lights assailed his senses. The bright, intrusive lights clipped past his foggy perspective as the EMS crew wheeled his near dead body down a long hallway towards a waiting surgical team. People were yelling, commanding sharp instructions at one another as they dragged him off the stretcher, and put him on an exam table.

More lights were turned on him. A stethoscope listened. He sensed an X-ray plate sliding under his body, as frantic hands used shears to cut away his tattered, bloody clothes. The hands touching his body weren't interested in comforting him. They had a very serious task at hand, and it would all be decided by what they did, or didn't do as doctors, and nurses. They worked fast, but were thorough. Billy saw through the crowd he was inside of a large white room somewhere inside of the hospital his father used to bring him in when his Asthma attacks got out of hand. He once came here for a routine surgery many years ago, but today, the situation was very dire, and it appeared Billy might succeed with his suicide plan if they couldn't undo the damage the bullet caused. He saw his friend from the Ambulance standing outside the trauma room. She smiled, turned, and didn't walk away, but she was gone, and vanished from his sight.

The nurses had cut off his blood soaked parka, muddy pants, leaving him shattered, and exposed to the world. He felt so broken, weak, and afraid. His friend was gone, and with her the warm, peace he felt as if he slept within on the way to the hospital. He was now left to feel the full force of the trauma in this cold, unforgiving trauma room, but this was where his life would end, or go on. Though Billy did not like this room, it had one purpose. Not everyone who came into this room, left alive, and by his actions today, regrettably, Billy put his life in the balance. This was Billy's turn on the table, and would he leave the table alive? Would he see the morning sunrise?

He felt as if his body, and spirit were attached to a fraying tether, and the hands working on him were desperately keeping him on this side of life. He felt gravity fade away. It was a voyage, a place to go once the string was cut, but the hands working on him were denying the voyage to the other side.

They started cutting into him.

He knew he had to be strong if he wanted to stay.

"Hold him! This is going to hurt!" A stern voice commanded from somewhere as those hands grabbed onto him harder, and resisted his urge to try and fight back against the pain.

That voice was right. It hurt.

Billy regretted suicide. This was the reality of it.

The pressure to his side caused by the trauma surgeon was worse than any pain he'd felt before. He tried to remember the good things he learned in the woods. He remembered love, hope, and reasons to live. He had to walk through this valley so he could live again, and experience the joy of loving others.

God had a purpose for Billy. So he had to be brave, and rest in his plans. God heard Billy's prayers, because He always hears, even when Billy didn't think God heard him.

There was no sense of time anymore. He felt a distant, violent compression to his chest. Hands were thrusting on him. He wanted to get off this table, and run away from those hands as they pounded on his chest.

He felt okay. They could let go of him.

Billy wanted to remain near the love, and sunlight he felt.

The room felt full of sunshine, and it was no longer cold, or impersonal.

He thought of his friend from the back of the ambulance, and knew she was near as well. He wanted to tell them it was no longer necessary to pound on his chest, or hold him to the table, or room with the ugly artificial light, because the warm sunshine was much more welcoming, and peaceful. What they were doing as they tried to save his life, seemed to still register. It felt violating. Violent. A desperate battle to keep him alive.

They weren't giving up on their sixteen year old patient. He had his whole life ahead of him and they wanted to save him.

The sunshine was warm, and he sensed he was pulling away from the artificial light, and letting go of that fraying chord that held him to his broken body.

The curtain to that moment in the past went down, and the gym lights were slowly back on as the song from the past ended. Bill finished his dance with his wife.

"Thank you for the dance," Erika said as she hugged Bill close. "We can go home now."

Bill jumped at the chance to leave this haunted place, and go back to the familiar, safe bubble he felt safe within.

He took a few minutes to say, "Take Care, let's stay in touch," with a few people as he collected their coats.

He'd seen enough.

It was time to leave those ghostly memories. Reaching the gym door, he held it open for Erika as he turned. He looked one last time, fully aware now...*the ghosts weren't inside of a brick, and mortar building.* They were frozen, stuck inside him.

There were no ghosts within a brick and mortar building. The ghosts were going to follow him, because of the trauma he survived.

He needed support.

Help from professionals who could help him process.

Bill no longer saw teenagers from yesterday, but before walking out, he paused and waved one last time to today's adults.

He could see today, clearer than ever.

He was a survivor. The scars, visible, and invisible were a testimony of his survival. Bill understood, many do not survive. Billy walked away from the brutality of a self-inflicted gunshot wound and near death in a trauma room.

Twenty years later, he had the gift of free will.

Life meant liberty, and liberty meant he could choose to be grateful right now for the gift of life and for the ones who loved him.

He could count his blessings.

Billy experienced what it felt like to breathe his last. But instead of the finality of death, he was given the extraordinary gift of life. Billy learned what really mattered in life.

The intangibles.

He could also choose to seek and accept help.

He could choose to be grateful in all circumstances.

He had agency to choose the path he would take, each, and every day he woke up alive.

Chapter Eight

Bill closed the gym door behind him. It was time to go home. If they got home in time, he would have time to see his kids before they went to bed. He wanted to hug them, and kiss them goodnight before they went to bed. He felt alive, and the smell of fresh, cold winter air tasted sweet. It tasted like life. If they got home in time, he would also have time to entertain his kids with stories from, *"The Silly Brown Bear Gang."*

The *Silly Brown Bear Gang*, was a hodge-podge group of stuffed animals Bill brought to life each night before bed with animated stories, and general shenanigans he brought to life. Each stuffed animal had their own personality, and every night Bill tucked his kids in after creating a happy, loving space for them. He used the stuffed critters to tell stories, wrestle with, and have pillow fights with until everyone was laughing, and smiling.

This was something he was grateful for, and something he chose to share with his kids. Bill prided himself as a father, because his kids didn't just go to bed. He alone was the only one who could bring the Silly Brown Bear Gang to Life.

The experience in the woods with Billy remained dormant for now within him as he counted his blessings, and grounding himself. Bill started the night, forgetting, but now he remembered, and he felt rich, grateful for life.

Back in their car. The tired, old motor tapped away as he remembered the same *day-to-day* strain from a few hours before.

The rat race.

The grind.

The bills.

Depression.

However, something had changed, because he remembered what was forgotten. He had the same problems, but a different perspective. He allowed life's stresses to drain the joy of living.

Bill remembered the joy Billy felt when he woke up alive!

All of those horrific reasons he chose to use suicide as a means to flee those reasons appeared to still be there when he woke up alive, but it didn't matter in that moment. All Billy cared about was the fact he was alive. There were Angels that day who intervened.

As Billy lay dying, what he wanted most was love. He understood he could give love away, even if others weren't showing it to him, Billy could give his love to others. He experienced what it was like to lose the liberty of life after pulling the trigger. There was no coming back from that suicidal moment. Suicide had almost denied him the chance to sit, and feel the anticipation of running home to his kids inside of a tired, old worn car with a knocking engine. It was his choice to not allow his anxiety, fears, and other circumstances rob him of the joy of living.

If Billy had succeeded in his attempt, and not fought that struggle to survive, there would be no Silly Brown Bear Gang. Billy grew up, and became a loving, decent person. That mattered.

"I think you've been too hard on yourself tonight Bill," Erika said as she looked patiently at her husband. "Don't compare yourself to the words you were raised under. You are here with us today, because you decided to fight back. I know this wasn't easy, maybe this is a step towards healing?"

Bill remained quiet, and listened.

"I hear your nightmares, and see the torment of those flashbacks at times. You're a good man, and we love you."

Bill smiled.

She was right.

He survived, but never started to heal. He was told by his father to, *"not do something like that again."* He also told him to *"move on from it."* Billy was expected to move forward as if it never happened.

Bill forgot what it felt like to wake up, so grateful for life.

He received a death pardon that Friday night. A second chance at life, but over time circumstances, and time clouded his sense of gratitude for the joy of living, and life.

Bill did experience a reunion.

He also understood he felt an obligation, and he wanted to be a good steward of the life he'd been given, but he got lost on the way. He was busy chasing after things that didn't really matter, and forgot life was about the intangibles.

"...it's not about what we leave behind, but what we take with us."

He needed help with his childhood trauma. His father's harsh words, and unforgiving expectations created within Bill the feeling, *he was never enough.*

He heard a lot about success over dinner at the reunion, and Bill felt lost in the grind, and rat race. But life was not what he earned. It wasn't about what he accumulated, or how comfortable he made things for his family.

A good steward was a grateful steward.

In a little, or a lot, a good life steward counted his blessings, and took care of what God had entrusted for the day.

God gave Bill life.

The distortion of suicide, and mental illness created by his trauma caused him to believe in that by taking his life, he would alleviate his suffering, but what it did was change his perspective, and show him what he actually surrendered.

Lying in the hospital bed for a few days Billy watched a national tragedy unfold on television. Without warning, an explosion lit up the television screen as several brave astronauts perished during the Space Shuttle Challenger disaster just three days after Billy almost died.

In some unexpected, empathic reality; Billy had a shared understanding where those astronauts were moments after it became obvious they perished.

Before that Friday night when Billy discharged a firearm intentionally at himself, people died. He heard about their deaths in the news, and he attended a few funerals, but Billy never made the same connection as he watched the astronauts from the Space Shuttle Challenger tragically leave this world.

He didn't understand why the experience felt so familiar. Everyday people were passing from this life, but he never felt a sensitivity to a shared experience until he woke up alive in the hospital, and watched the Challenger incident.

"...they went further than me," Billy heard those words as clear as a bell inside of his thoughts as the nurses stood in shock like the rest of the nation, and watched helplessly.

It was a voyage, and he intuitively felt the perishing astronauts traveled onward while the harsh hands in the trauma kept him from moving on. There was a place full of peaceful sunlight, bathed in two different lights. A light of serene peace, and the brutal, artificial lights of a trauma room. There were two distinct places, and to go anywhere, you must undertake a voyage, or journey.

The nurses, and doctors like the rest of the nation were shaken by the unexpected disaster, but no one spoke to Billy about the suicide attempt that nearly took his life. His near fatal attempt happened on a Friday, and the Challenger disaster happened on live TV on Tuesday. Billy was only regaining complete consciousness that Tuesday morning.

That night as the nation mourned, and asked questions, Billy saw the woods all over again. He saw the terrifying *flash-bang* of the muzzle blast after he discharged the firearm, and it made him want to claw his way out of his own skin to escape the flashback. He was immobile in a hospital bed, attached to IVs, and a chest tube. There were gauze pads covering his wounds, hiding the bullet scar. He would see, and smell things that were not there, and use his pillow to try, and hide from reliving the things that happened in the woods.

Long after the shooting as Billy grew into Bill he could still smell, and taste the bitter taste of gunpowder as he tried to mow grass, or brush his teeth.

The day after the Space Shuttle Challenger disaster the surgeon came to see Billy. He wanted Billy to follow up with him after discharge. Medicines were prescribed for pain, and medicine to help him sleep, and not see the *flash-bang* for a few nights. There were antibiotics prescribed, and though his face was battered, and swollen there was nothing the doctor could do. He reassured Billy that in a week, or two he would be able to see again from his left eye, and reminded him that he smashed his face against a tree, and dragged it over many yards of rugged terrain as he fought for his life.

"That is the least of your concerns son," the doctor said. "You're alive, and most do not come back. It was not your time when they brought you to see me."

Billy felt numb.

"You were given a gift," he said as he patted Billy on the leg, and finished his assessment.

Harsh words were exchanged between the surgeon, and Billy's father, because the doctor insisted Billy have access to a therapist, and Psychiatrist. His father scoffed, incensed that the doctor was pushing it as they debated on the other side of the closed hospital curtain.

His father reluctantly agreed. It wouldn't last, because after a few visits, his father stopped taking him to see the Psychiatrist.

Leaving the hospital, Billy felt like a scarecrow. His clothes hung from his thin body, and he was covered in scars. He was a survivor.

The nightmares, and flashbacks would follow Billy home, and back to school. He felt as if the vibrant images were like living inside of a possessed time machine. They weren't the same as memories. Some nights he woke up sweating, and he wanted to hide under his pillow to get away from the sight of the gun, or crawl away from what happened next. He felt it in his hands. The deliberate steps he took the night as he loaded, removed the safety, turned the firearm, and pointed it at himself.

Billy remembered the Bible in his bedroom. He remembered God heard him. He never left Billy. There was a gentle, reassuring comfort in that as the flashbacks lied, and tried to tell him he was in the woods again. Billy was able to sleep as he rested in what he learned about the nature of God, because for now, the nightmares left.

Chapter Nine

A week after Billy was sent home from the hospital there was a random telephone call. The caller asked to speak to Billy, despite Billy's father's confusion, he handed Billy the phone, and said, "It's some lady on the phone, and she wants to talk to you."

"Hello," Billy said into the phone.

A bright, pleasant voice greeted Billy from the other end. The caller was the mother of a friendly girl who sat behind Billy in homeroom class. Over the years Billy had developed a friendly rapport with the girl, but never went so far as to meet her mother. The caller said she had a very important message for him, and she wanted to know if they could meet soon?

"I know it sounds crazy Billy," she began after introducing herself. "I was vacuuming my house, and above the sound of my loud vacuum cleaner I heard someone speak to me. I had to shut off my vacuum, so I could listen. I know, I probably sound crazy, because right now you're probably asking yourself, *'who's this crazy lady calling?'*" Her name was Linda, and she was cheerful, vibrant, and it made him smile.

"Billy to be honest, you've never been in my thoughts before, and I'm sure this must be awkward for you, but I have to say to you, what was spoken to me. Are you okay with that?" Linda asked.

"Sure," Billy replied into the phone. He was curious, but felt an instant connection to the vibe he felt from his instant, unlikely new friend.

Linda laughed, and made another reference about sounding like some kind of *"crazy cat lady,"* before she continued.

"God loves you Billy. I believe he would like for me to come see you soon, if that is okay?"

He wanted to be near God. After waking up alive in the hospital, he only felt safe when he felt a closeness with God. It seemed to Billy only God comforted him when the nightmares from the woods haunted his dreams, and made him afraid to go to sleep at night. When darkness came, and the woods loomed not far from his bedroom window, only God stilled the fear of the darkness shrouding the woods. The haunting memory of feeling the presence of death forming in those final, labored breaths.

He agreed to visit his new friend in a few days.

Several days later Linda came to visit Billy's house as he continued to recover from his wounds. She rolled into their driveway in a bright yellow station wagon, with wood paneling. Billy grinned, because of course, this cheerful soul would drive a yellow station wagon, trimmed with brown paneling.

Billy's father opened the door, and let her inside. She came with ice cream, a smile, and a Bible.

After introducing herself formally to Billy, and his family, his father left them alone in the living room for an hour.

After they shared small talk, and ice cream, Linda opened her Bible, and shared once more the story about the other day when she was busy doing chores around her home, and heard what she believed was the unmistakable voice of God. Perhaps, in another time, and place, Billy would have thought she was a little *"off"*, but after what he just experienced just over a week ago, nothing surprised him.

She left that afternoon, and Billy became close friends with Linda, and the rest of her family.

Billy's father never put him back in the chair, or put his hands on him. He stopped verbally breaking him down, and allowed him to socialize, and live an active life outside of their home. However, his father remained steadfast, and refused to continue to take Billy to see a therapist, or Psychiatrist. Billy had to learn to live with the trauma, and act *as if it never happened.*

So with the passing of the years, and time the gunshot was not as loud as it once was. The unbearable, suffocating smells of blood, and gunpowder bothered him a little less. He got used to the aches, and pains of the bullet scar next to his heart.

What replaced surviving childhood trauma became paying the responsibilities of adult living. He brought the trauma with him as he married a girl, and soon had three babies in a busy family. They bought a car, a house, adopted some dogs, and life started happening every day.

Bill felt as if life were burying him the older he got. The critical words he measured himself with as a father were the same words he heard growing up. Billy was gone by now, and Bill became a husband, father, and a struggling provider. Diapers, electric bills, and working tirelessly to provide became his day-to-day life. Each day the strain of the grind felt as if a brick were added to the wall that separated him from the valued lessons he learned about life the night he almost died. He felt the physical pains of his scars almost daily, but their significance, and what they meant was often shoved aside.

Bill lost the joy of living.

He forgot the feeling of the solemn gratitude for life.

He remembered what it felt like to wake up alive, and breathe the sweet air of life.

"...You were as close to gone as anyone can be, without being gone forever Billy."

Those were the surgeon's words. He knew how close Billy was to succeeding at his suicide attempt. Billy came within a few minutes of succeeding in his attempt, and if he had, he would have died regretting his attempt.

The greatest news Billy ever heard was the news he would survive his suicide attempt. A reprieve. A pardon from an act he fought to undo. He was allowed to leave the courtroom of consequences as a free man the night he got a second chance at life. Bill remembered it was probably human nature to take things for granted until we were at risk for losing them forever. As long as Bill was alive he had agency, and freedom to choose how he would respond to life. A change in his perspective put him on a new course once before. He had the same circumstances, but what changed was his perspective about life.

Suicide felt like a wall Billy had to climb. That wall of life was his fear of serious harm, and death. It took time for him to plan, get comfortable with the decision, shop for means and resources, and finally accept his decision.

There were no more "cries for help."

A faux peace settled over him.

But once he succeeded and made that near fatal attempt, crossing over, he experienced the totality of consequences.

As he tried to climb back over the wall of consequences it became a savage battle for survival.

Billy prayed once before, and asked God to send an Angel to help him. That was not a one time offer from God. Sitting in his driveway on a snowy night, Bill remembered where he came from. His experience also taught him that he was stronger than he could ever imagine. He was alive, right now, and so right now, he could choose how to respond to life's circumstances. The things he could control.

He saw Erika, and his kids through the living room window. The house had a warm, inviting glow. Twenty six years after his near fatal suicide attempt, he was safe, alive, and living his best life. He needed help, and help was available, because he was still suffering trauma.

The kids were eagerly waiting for the *Silly Brown Bear Gang,* and that was living. He had the freedom to go inside, hug his kids, and regale them with silly stories from an eclectic collection of stuffed animals.

This was the present. This was not the home he grew up in. His life was just steps away, waiting for him. Once more Bill felt the joy of waking up alive!

Bill heard the voice of an old friend. A familiar voice who once spoke to him in the woods. He smiled as he watched the snow collect on the windshield.

"Would you exchange the life you have now, for another?"

He knew the answer.

God granted Bill his heart's desire. As he lay dying, Billy didn't express a desire for fame, or riches, or success.

"...Love, we take love with us when we die," he replied to the familiar voice.

"...That's a good answer, be grateful, and now go and live."

He had so much to be grateful for, and suddenly the burdens he carried no longer felt heavy as he stepped from his van, and headed towards. He could hear the sound of his children as they ran to see their father. Bedtime was a big production in Bill's house, because it was time for the Silly Brown Bear Gang. Bill would gladly accept the trials of life if it meant he could live in the love he had all around him. He remembered one night laying in the woods, afraid he would never see another sunrise.

Twenty years later, his kids were mobbing him.

Covered by their hugs, and laughter, it felt good to be alive.

They missed their dad tonight as they eagerly waited for the Silly Brown Bear Gang. Bill picked up his daughter, and hugged her tightly. His boys grabbed his legs, and held on as they shrieked with laughter.

"Can we play Silly Brown Bear?" Autumn asked.

"Of course," Bill said.

Bill sat her on the couch, as he picked Beau up, and smiled at his sticky, ice cream coated face, and remembered a laughter he once heard, many years ago, in the past.

"What have you been eating?" Bill asked.

"Ice Cream," Beau replied.

"...I'm alive," Bill reminded himself, *"Is there any greater gift than life?"*

Bill had lost his way. It's easy to do sometimes in life, to forget what matters. He reminded himself that the remedy for that is to remain grateful, because as long as he's alive, he can change his perspective, and go another way.

"Okay guys, tell Belinda goodnight, and let's head upstairs to bed!" Bill said as Erika walked their neighbor to the door.

"Let's fly dad!" Beau said as he held his arms out wide as if they were the wings of an airplane.

"Contact!" Bill said as he hoisted his son into the air.

"Contact!" Beau replied as he mimicked airplane noises.

"Let's fly son."

A distant memory pulls back the curtain of time as Billy pedals his bike over dusty summer roads. His imagination carries him high above the clouds, banking the wings of his airplane freely into the wind, and feeling the lift of freedom from the sad, dark home he lived in.

"We're going to be okay Billy...I promise," Bill thought to himself as he flew his young son up the stairs and did his best to mimic the sound of an airplane gaining altitude.

Bill flew Beau towards bed as Christian, and Autumn ran after their dad. Soon the eclectic band of stuffed critters were out in force entertaining his three happy, healthy children as their father lovingly tucked them in.

Once they were asleep. Bill bowed his head, and whispered a gracious word of *thanks* to God, for the life he'd been given, because he understood that in the trials, and difficulties, God never abandoned him, and in the sufferings of life, it made him the person he was today....

www.ingramcontent.com/pod-product-compliance
Lightning Source LLC
LaVergne TN
LVHW022232200926
848481LV00006B/2230